Praise for *The Power of JAH Will*

This powerful work by C. W. Eddy is like talking to a wise, old friend who shares fascinating tidbits of church history that help explain the traditions and customs of the Christian faith. For, perhaps, the first time in your life, Dr. Eddy's book will cause you to pause and think about hell, religion, life, and our Creator. His thought-provoking work will cause those who are frustrated with religion to cheer and will likely ruffle the feathers of others (just the way I like it). It reminds me of that old childhood taunting: "truth hurts, doesn't it?" But if we know God's true character, *The Power of JAH Will* is good medicine for the soul.

~ Larry Broughton—Serial Entrepreneur—
US Army Special Forces Veteran

The Power of JAH Will is all about relationship. My relationship with "Chuck" spans over four decades dating back to Anderson College in the '70s. After many years of lost contact we have recently been reunited through the magic of social media. I must tell you that I am both surprised and impressed with the work God is doing through my old college roommate, not only as a minister, counselor, and missionary, but also as an author and a good one at that. Yes, C. W. will both entertain and challenge you with this new book based upon the Hebrew roots of our Christian faith. Listen to C. W., as Yahweh's messenger, call His church and each of us individually back to a true faith based upon our Jewish roots. You will not be disappointed.

~ Doug Seelbach, Ph.D.
Professor of Kinesiology
Anderson University

I have known C. W. Eddy for many years. Chuck loves to have deep and meaningful "faith conversations." He brings this desire into his most recent book *The Power of JAH Will*. Written as though he is sitting across from you in comfortable surroundings, Chuck will encourage you to objectively revisit the fundamentals of faith. The discussion will take you into the domain of history and back into the realm of absolutes as found in the Word of God. In doing so C. W. Eddy will encourage the reader to "magnify the power and the will of Jehovah" with him.

~ Dr. David Herne, Heritage AFlame Ministries

C. W. Eddy's book, *The Power of JAH Will*, is a fitting next step from his first book, The Power of I Will. He provides unique insight into God's work within the Jewish nation, the early history of Christ's Church, and religious history since that time. Building upon the theme of "will," he brings us back to the basis of our lives here on this planet—the supreme will of God and the love of God for all mankind. Not only does he provide thought-provoking historical information and often comical present-day analogies, his book forced me to re-examine my own core beliefs and traditions, widely-held traditions and beliefs that have negatively affected the growth of His Church over the last 2000 years. I look forward to further delving into the resources and references Dr. Eddy provides in his book!

~ Todd J. Reynolds, M.D.

Well researched and interesting read by a long-time friend of mine. I may not have come to the same conclusions as him, but I always welcome the honest debate of ideas, and Chuck does a good job of laying out his ideas in a systematic and researched way.

~ Rev. Kurt Heisey – Pastor and Entrepreneur
President, Liberty Seamless Enterprises, Inc.

THE POWER OF
JAH WILL

For information about this title or to order other books and/or electronic media, contact the publisher:

Pilgrim-Way

www.journey-man.org

ISBN: 978-0-9832306-2-5 (print)
978-0-9832306-3-2 (eBook)

Cover and interior design: 1106 Design

Illustrations: Dore Bible Illustrations, *www.creationism.org/images/*

https://www.google.com/search?q=british+battle+formation+pictures&rlz

http://matadornetwork.com/trips/33-colossal-monuments-statues-around-world/ —Joe Batruny

All scripture was taken from the New International Version Bible.

RETURN TO INNOCENCE

THE POWER OF JAH WILL

C. W. EDDY

Dedication

To my dear wife, Angela, who continues to believe in me.

To the seeker . . . may we meet and worship together.

Table of Contents

Author's Note

*T*here once was a time in the history of mankind when knowledge was passed on by pictures or by oral tradition. There have been periods when the common man was kept away from truth and enlightenment by cultural elite, ruthless dictators, elevated clergy and even mystics. People of the past were often kept in ignorance or were assumed to not be able to understand the very things that might set them free.

We now live in an age where people have almost instant access to virtual libraries and treasuries of the accumulated wisdom and history of man. Oftentimes in their maddening rush to learn, uncover or sort through the avalanche of information, they demand the "condensed" version. This is not a good time in history to be an encyclopedia salesman. Indeed, some who read this may not even know what that occupation was. Many of our parents never dreamed of a day when handwritten letters would give way to emails, which are already being replaced by text messages, tweets, instagrams, and perhaps with holograms soon to follow!

In my humble opinion we already have "hollow-grams" . . . . far too much empty information and chatter.

With this in mind you will find that I write in a bit of a "less is more" style. Today's seeker is not an idiot. If she or he finds a topic of intrigue or connection, they will use whatever means at hand to search it out and build upon it. I have been told by many who have read my work that they find it almost conversational. In fact some who also know me say they can almost hear my voice as they read along.

"What's up with the geese?"

The word migrate can mean to move, either permanently or seasonally, from one place to another. Whether of our own will or the call of nature, we are being called "homeward." May this book be a key in the freedom to follow that call.

🪶 🪶 🪶

"Great truths and true friends are much alike—if you find even a few, and they last through life—you are blessed."

—C. W. Eddy

Introduction

"Never before in the history of mankind . . . yada, yada, yada." I am suspicious when I come across an article or opinion that leads out with such a broad brush statement. I'm leery for several reasons. I know I'm getting old, but to speak authoritatively about things that happened long before I came into existence can get me into trouble. And speaking about getting older, I see things in such a different light as I age that sometimes I have to rethink my position. Also, we live in an age of such cynicism. You name the topic or opinion and I guarantee that almost instantly I can find a counter and often opposite position on it. It seems as though EVERY issue we might gallantly take sides on can be met with people who vehemently oppose it. And I am speaking here of people with good intentions. Not the ones who purposely revise history to fit their agenda or those who are just plain antagonistic.

So let's start with something basic and see if we can find agreement. Why do people write? I have to ask myself this as I begin this book. I mean really, why in this day and age, do so many continue to write? Ok, here I go . . . "Never before in the history of man have there been so many writers." Do you know what? That might actually be accurate. There are hundreds of thousands of writers of books alone. Not to mention millions of tabloid and magazine writers . . . and let's not forget hundreds of millions of blogs in this day and age. So why bother? There are several reasons really and I need to face each one if I am going to persevere through this ordeal while still trying to keep you with me.

I am quite a realist I suppose. I think I deal with probabilities well and frame some of my efforts accordingly.

Why do we write?

1. Do I write to become rich or famous? Well I have written before and am *underwhelmed* with the response. I became neither rich nor famous. And being a student of history as well as a realist, I am not convinced that either of those outcomes would benefit me. When I look at the bulk of people who have reached what the world usually acclaims as rich or famous, I see a long wake of broken humanity washed up along the shore. Many have ridden a wave of fame and glory only to have self-destructed during or soon after their rise to the top. Furthermore, if I am candid with myself, I find those who have touched me the most deeply during my life journey had VERY little by means of power, possessions, or prestige. How about you? What is the nature of the people who have touched you the most?

2. I write to change the world. Now that must sound posi-tively arrogant. What can someone the likes of you and I

do to change the world? I am a Christian man. Although you may or may not be, you might at least call yourself "spiritual." I believe in a personal God . . . a creative God, and that we are created in His image. So that means to me that we MUST be creative to feel at all fulfilled. Someone once said, "We are not human beings—here on a spiritual journey. Rather we are spiritual beings—here on a human journey." I like that quote very much. I dare to believe that something you or I do can have impact upon the world we live in. Here goes another "never before" statement. Never before in the history of the world have people consumed as much as they do now. Do you think that is valid? People consume more food, more products, more music, and more information than perhaps at any time in world history. And yet are we more happy . . . more fulfilled? I just saw something ridiculous in the news today. Students were DEMANDING that their colleges provide cafeteria meals that were culturally diverse and sensitive. Let me get this straight. These cupcakes applied to the university of their choice . . . purchased a meal ticket plan for its convenience and affordability . . . and then want to boycott the school for their political incorrectness? That is almost as absurd as immigrants who are rescued as they come across our borders illegally, demanding that they be served meals that are in keeping with their national cuisine and tastes. I told you I write in a conversational style and you just caught me chasing a squirrel. Sorry about that!

Writing gives us a chance to turn the tides on consumerism. Rather than consume more, we can make something. Isn't that exciting? Every day, when you put your fingers to the keys, you're creating something. And then, with the click of a button, you can share it with the world.

Humans have a built-in need to make our mark on the world. We want to bring new things to life, to mold things into the image we have in our imaginations, to subdue the earth. We write not just to change the world, but to create a new world.[1]

—Joe Bunting

3. I write because I HOPE. That may be a bit confusing to you. Let me explain. The psychiatrist Victor Frankl posited that the main search of mankind is not happiness or pleasure but meaning. "Life is never made unbearable by circumstances, but only by lack of meaning and purpose," he wrote in *Man's Search for Meaning*.[2] I do agree with him. I am probably not alone when I suggest to you that, within each of us, we play subliminal recordings of earlier childhood perceptions or expectations. We who are parents can all remember our little ones crying out, "look Daddy . . . watch me Daddy . . . Look Mommy look," as they tried to throw a ball, ride a bike, or dance before our eyes. I would suggest to you that each of us, still in some way, may at times resemble that little child who says, "Look Daddy/Mommy—see what I have become or done in my life." Again, I somewhat agree with Frankl's quote, but because of my love for the Holy Scripture I go a little further in my search and foundation.

A few paragraphs ago I opined that never before in the history of man has so much been consumed, and yet would any of us declare that never before has man been so satisfied? We consume but do we savor? We fill up with all manner of things, but are we fulfilled? Ecclesiastes tells us:

> "Whoever loves money never has enough. Whoever has wealth is never satisfied with his income. This too is meaningless. As goods increase, so do those who consume them."
>
> —Ecclesiastes 5:10

I wrote earlier that we live in a time of unprecedented advances in science, technology and communication. But I do not necessarily agree that we live in unprecedented times. Solomon tells us that really there is nothing new under the sun. He speaks a great deal about vanity and true meaning. I think that while many of the "stage props" reflect the times we live in . . . the *"play"* is much the same throughout history.

> "Then I realized that it is good and proper for a man to eat and drink and find satisfaction in his toilsome labor under the sun during his few days of life God has given him—for this is his lot. Moreover, when God gives any man wealth and possessions and enables him to enjoy them, to accept his lot and be happy in his work—this is a gift of God."
>
> —Ecclesiastes 5:18-20

So, for those who write, let them write because in doing so it resonates with their creative nature. Let us who hope, do so believing that we, even such as we, can inspire or guide others. If we are not so cynical to believe that we change during our lives, we must acknowledge that we have changed in great measure by something we learned, read, or interfaced with—if only an idea—that was created in the mind of someone before us. I dare say that your reasons for reading may have some similar motivations. The depressive personality, or those who despair, usually do not participate in even these simple and basic activities. To read or write is to stay **engaged** in the affairs of life. Without perhaps even recognizing it, this demonstrates HOPE. We hope that we might find meaning, that we may affect change in others and in ourselves. I challenge you to keep at it. I hope you continue on through this book and in our conversation. "Stay thirsty my friend."

Many years ago in an early stage of my life I was a high school teacher. I remember in my Psychology class, I tried to keep my students engaged while observing their behavior. I would, during the course of a semester, give them some brain teasers. I was always amazed at how some ate it up and wanted more. But there were many others who pulled down the shades of their mind or imagination. They gave up so early and so easily. I know similarly that in the course of writing a book such as this that I will lose some. Some would have me spell out every thought to almost take any thinking on their part out of the equation. Some will enjoy a condensed version and do their own further research on topics of interest. And some . . . yeesh . . . they dropped out long ago. That's too bad, because I was just going to give a little "pop quiz." Do you notice a certain word missing in the following statement?

Sometimes people can seem oblivious to the most basic things of importance. Missing the central message entirely, they make things far more confusing than they were originally intended to be.

Did you find it? What—are you stupid? It was right there in front of you. I told you what to look for. Do I have to write it a different way? OK . . . . Do you notice a certain word—**missing**—in the previous statement above? If you are not mad at me for playing with you, I invite you to find a brain teaser at the end of each chapter. Ignore it if you're not into that sort of thing. They will graduate in difficulty from "T-ball" to the Varsity level. They will have nothing to do with the book and you will not get a grade at the end. ☺

I included this little quiz just to make a point to build upon. Each of us has different learning styles and communication preferences. You are soon to enter a book . . . a discussion . . . that is designed to make you think. It is my intent to have US look at several things that are of utmost importance, and try to look at them through a different lens or perspective. You are not about to read a novel, love story, or a cook book. Those three genres are best sellers. They dominate the vast majority of book sales. But I told you that what we are going to enter into is of utmost importance. Indeed, wars have been fought over what we may touch upon.

I will try to make our visit interesting. I do hope you will take your time reading this book and let some things *marinate.*

Chapter 1
What's in a Name?

*H*ave you ever made a mistake? Of course you have. Have you ever felt the need to correct it, if that was even possible? My first book is called *The Power of I Will*. Of course I am biased, but I think it is quite good. It is not like this one in many respects in that I use a lot of apologetics in it. I used many facts or defenses of my position to get people to look at why they believe what they say they believe. Of course I proofread it and then sent it along to an editor to do the same. After it went into print, I learned that one of the statements I made as fact turned out to be not altogether true. It was something I had been taught and it was quoted to me in one of the books I had been tested upon during graduate years. I debated whether to correct it or just leave it, feeling that only I alone would probably even notice or challenge the statement. I finally knew that I would rest better if I made the revision. It takes time and money to revise a book once it has been published. I contacted the publisher of both printed and e-book versions and I'm now satisfied with my work. My name

1

is on it. What does that even mean? To have "your name" on something implies that your reputation, your integrity, perhaps even your authority is involved.

What do you have your name on?

We all are on a journey in this life. To denounce or reject that is to miss out on one of the most basic truths in life. I once spent some years learning martial arts. The Grandmaster of *AKT Combatives*[3] developed a Student Creed. One of the tenets of that creed at the dojo I attended, and the style he developed, is this . . . "Evolve or become irrelevant." If we have our eyes open at all we see this born out in society or the market place. Many of you who are reading this have no idea what an eight-track used to be. You scramble around to buy gadgets and download your music onto devices that have built-in obsolescence. A new device or medium is sure to come along that will make your treasure into another generation's relic. Did you know that there was a time when a "party line" was cutting-edge technology? Never mind . . . you don't know what that is either.

Why is it that we have such a stinking hard time allowing ourselves to look at and examine some of the most basic things we BELIEVE? I am not telling you that you have to change. Some things should be believed and remain central even as the world evolves and spins around them. I recommend you get a copy of *The Power of I Will*.[4] It is a good book and makes a great catalyst for discussion or study. But, while I am basically satisfied with the work, I find that I have grown some, perhaps evolved, in some areas of belief. If there is one thing I feel I over-emphasized, it is that of our personal free will. Don't get me wrong. I still believe that is HUGE. It is still fundamental and perhaps the most precious attribute God has given to his creation. But in magnifying or concentrating so much upon that, I feel I diminished in some way the power of **God's** will—a power that is light years, so to speak, beyond ours. Not to mention that it is God who created light . . . and years . . . and us!!

I told you I am a pragmatic type of guy. In case you forgot just what that means, let me give you a definition:

> *Pragmatic—adjective. 1. of or relating to a practical point of view or practical considerations. 2. treating historical phenomena with special reference to their causes, antecedent conditions, and results.*

You might say I like to keep things simple. I just seemed to be wired that way. I get increasingly annoyed with people who want to draw others into mysticism, special knowledge, or elite-ism by their desire to complicate things. I am what you might call a Christian. I do not for a minute think, that in being so, it means I had to check my intellect at the door. My first book gives compelling evidence that demands a verdict in the case for creation as well as the Christ—the Author—of that creation. And yet when I read the Holy Scripture, I find that this Jesus was a master of getting to the bottom line. He spoke in parables often in his teaching—simple lessons—and story telling. Instead of quoting scripture that truly speaks of HIM, or banging people over the head with a "hundred pound Torah," he often tried to reduce the Kingdom of God to its most common denominator. The Jewish faith had hundreds of commandments to follow. Many were commandments given by God himself, and too many others were the "commandments of men." Jesus cut to the chase when religious leaders of the day tried to trap him into something blasphemous and trip him in matters of the Law.

Hearing that Jesus had silenced the Sadducees, the Pharisees got together. One of them, an expert in the Law, tested him with this question: Teacher, which is the greatest commandment in the Law?

Jesus replied: "Love the Lord your God with all your heart and with all your soul and with all your mind. This is the first and greatest commandment. And the second is like it. Love your neighbor as yourself. All of the Law and the prophets hang on these two commandments."

—Matthew 22:34-40

So I say all that to say this: in my opinion, in our day and age, things are too complicated. Our beliefs need to change and change for the better. The subtitle of my book says "Return to innocence." I love that concept. Do you recall a time in your childhood when things seemed simple or better defined? Was there ever a time when you were just plain innocent . . . maybe even more alive? It is my intention to help us find our way—not back—but **to**—a place of joy and simplicity . . . with our eyes fully open and not in denial, and yet to a position of greater certainty about those things which truly matter most.

Before we go on, can we take just a little exercise in imagination? Imagine that you are on your way back home from work or school. As you get closer to your house you notice thick black smoke rising up in the sky. There are sirens blaring, and first responders are bustling all around your house or apartment. You are frantic. You rush toward the scene. One of the firemen gets hold of you and assures you that NOBODY is inside. There is no person or pet that you need fear is trapped inside. The authority senses your composure and returns to putting out the blaze. Yet you still wish you could run in and get something before the fire engulfs your precious dwelling. If you could—what might you risk going back in for? You might even write a response in the space below.

One of the roles I am involved with these days is that of a chaplain. I have the blessing to be involved with many wonderful elders who are in an assisted-living complex in our city. All have already had to face the loss of loved ones and many the loss of a child. All have had to face the trauma of downsizing from a home they loved, full of special memories as well as memorabilia. I have used the above imagination exercise with this group as well as in a seminar setting with a younger crowd. I found that more of those in what I call "Elderhood" had an answer that was aligned with mine than in settings made up largely of younger adults. I will give you my answer and of course state that it makes me no better or more spiritual than you if yours is different. I would go back into the blaze to retrieve my bible—the bible I have used for almost twenty years. It has been my journal. It has names and dates scribbled in it. It has places underlined and comments I have made—even arguments with God. The pages are worn and most have some staining from the oils on my hands as I have used it. I have taken it with me to several nations as I have been called to preach and teach.

Children are wonderful . . . but they grow and cannot be contained in their beautiful pictures on my wall. They leave your nest as they should and forge lives of their own. Good health is truly a gift . . . but that weakens and fails us. Our possessions, which we worked so hard to accumulate, are burdensome and will not bring us comfort or answers to life's greatest tests. So—if I could . . . I would go back in for my bible. God's word is my greatest source of comfort, wisdom, and guidance through this journey I call "Soul School." And, if history repeats itself as it has so many times in the past (and powerful people try to take even my bible), I will have a large amount of treasure stored up in me where they cannot spoil.

I had to take us on that little exercise for the purpose of establishing a fundamental. I believe the word of God is inspired and divine. It is unique and powerful. It is unlike any other body of spiritual writing or opinion of man. And we are at a time in history when many are willing to kill us for even as much as the statement I just made above. So what's in a Name? That was the title of this chapter. I believe that we are in a time when we had better get an idea of under what "name" or group identity it is with which we choose to be affiliated. And this is not like my brain teaser exercise where you can participate or not. We are in an age when, like it or not, we WILL have to engage with the "conversation" around us. So let's get at it. This name I speak of is Jehovah. He alone is God. I marvel at how it is that Christians are about the only faith that is so eager to assimilate. I am a missionary to India as well as Africa. In India, the country is far and away Hindu. People are being killed and churches burned down due to religious persecution. It is preposterous for me to think I will meet a Hindu that tells me, "No problem—we all serve the same god. Shiva is the same as your Jehovah." In Africa, we see country after country that is moving toward Islam and even Sharia Law. I have never heard of, or met, a Muslim who is willing to invite me to the party and agree that Allah is the same as my God. You will not find a devout Jew who concedes that Jehovah is the same entity as any other god.

So I ask you to consider, what's in a Name? Scripture tells us that there is salvation in **no other name.** I revised a portion of my first book simply because my "name" was on it. My integrity, my reputation, and my authority were all connected to my belief and my action. Study sometime, the power in the Name of Jehovah and its unique attributes. I think you will be enlightened and amazed. It might even shed some light on one of those *dusty old notions* we refer to as the Ten Commandments and taking the Name of the Lord in vain. And so when I thought about the title of the sequel to my first book *The Power of I Will*, I considered: Who will I lose, who will I engage, or who will I honor? I titled it *The Power of JAH Will*. This is taken straight from Scripture. "Not in my bible," you may say. And no—even though I love Jamaica and the island people I have spent so much time with—I am not a Rastafarian. You might be surprised to learn that a version of scripture so many thought to be premier, the 1611 version of the King James Bible, used the word Jah. It has been used in other versions from time to time as well. It is taken from the most holy Name of God—the Hebrew YHVH. The tetragrammaton was written because the Name of God was so sacred that it was not even allowed to be mentioned. Later vowels were added from which we get Yahweh or Jehovah. I once was on a plane and struck up a conversation with an orthodox Jew. In passing I mentioned "Blessed be Ha Shem." He looked at me as if to say "how does this Gentile know that term?" Ha Shem means *The Name*—whereby they sometimes allude to God without speaking his holy name! When using this title for my book I want to bring honor to the One I believe to be most worthy. Worthy of all honor and the one true God. So please do not be offended or put off by my use of the Name—Jah. I won't stuff it down your throat. But I would like to suggest that you consider it and that it is indeed a title of our King. OK—you need more proof? Here then, as taken straight from Wikipedia!

Jah or **Yah** (Hebrew: יהּ *Yahu*) is a short form of Yahweh (in consonantal spelling YHWH; Hebrew: יהוה), the proper name of the God of Israel in the Hebrew Bible.[1] This short form of the name occurs 50 times in the text of the Hebrew Bible.

The abbreviated form Jah (/dʒɑː/)[31] or Yah (◀)ⁱ/jɑː/; יה, *Yahu*) appears in the Psalms[32] and Isaiah.[33] It is a common element in Hebrew theophoric names such as Elijah and also appears in the forms *yahu* ("Jeremiah"), yeho ("Joshua"), and yo ("John," ultimately from the biblical "Yohanan"). It also appears 24 times in the Psalms as a part of Hallelujah ("Praise Jah").⁵

As we move into the next chapter remember that the intent of this book is to to simplify and clarify some of the things we believe and hold dear.

🦆 🦆 🦆

* Oh yes—I mentioned we might have a little brain teaser at chapter's end. I have two coins in my pocket. They total thirty-five cents . . . . US currency, by the way. One of the coins is NOT A DIME. What are the two coins in my pocket? Answers are in the back.

Chapter 2

Early Church

*D*uring these next three chapters I will be giving you information I have used many times for leadership seminars in several countries. I will present the topics each time in a bit of a different role. In this chapter I hope to come to you after the fashion of a lawyer—trying to present a case. In the next one pertaining more to history, I may appear as more of a professor. And in chapter four I hope you let me appeal to you as a friend. At no time in our conversation or in the course of this book do I ask or demand you to believe me. I find that, when I sense a demand in a presenter, I tend to put up defenses which block learning.

As we get started, I would like you to pause for a minute. Really—stop running through the pages—and think of your opinion on the following question.

What about those Jews?

We must really have our heads buried in our **smart device** if we don't consider a question like this. Is it just some goofy coincidence that a nation about the size of New Jersey is in WORLD news daily? I mean really—who or what are they? Are they a race or is it a religion? Or can it be both? Were they perhaps once a sort of "chosen" group of people; but who blew it and threw away their position and favor with God due to their rejection of some Messiah? And what about you or I if we claim to be Christian; are we a whole different religion—and if so, is that Jehovah's plan or ours?

Well, there are many answers to questions in the last paragraph. Some feel being a Jew is just a religion, one of several major world religions, but nothing special in its own right. And since we are all on pretty much the same path, we will all reach a similar end. *And this, they feel, is God's will.* Some feel the Jews are a race of people that are abhorrent and deserve annihilation. They vow publicly and openly before the world that they will not be satisfied until every trace of them is erased from the face of the earth. *And this, they feel, is God's will.* Some feel that while God did give his laws and promises to this people group, they transferred all rights and promises to their brand of faith when they rejected Jesus as Messiah. They are positive that Israel has been **replaced** in the grand purpose of God. *And this, they feel, is God's will.*

I do believe there is one true God. His name is Jehovah. And I believe he has a will. I think that far too many people do or say things, claiming it is the "will of God." Therefore, I make the next statement with humility and reverence. I think there are some messages that Jah tries to convey to mankind during different seasons of history. And if I am candid with you, it seems when the light finally goes on in my head or heart and I embrace something like this, I find that I am way behind the learning curve! I must be such a hard-head. You may not be too surprised if I tell you that even though I travel and teach in many Third World countries, I do not feel one big heart cry of the Father is a *Prosperity Gospel.* I do, however, believe one message that He has tried to communicate to mankind, especially Christendom, is this: our need to understand our Jewish roots and connection.

As we continue in this chapter on the Early Church I will be presenting a case taken only from Holy Scripture. In fact, we will be taking all references out of the book of Acts. I want to present a case to you as to what this early church looked like. I will leave it up to you to weigh the evidence and deliver a verdict. I will list each scripture, but might not write the whole part down word for word. PLEASE take the time to look over each one to determine if I pulled them out of context or twisted their meaning.

We as believers can be so easily threatened and angered. If you study people like I do, you would be amazed at how few people who consider themselves Christian really know the scriptures. Oftentimes they see one another at their place of worship and might generally assume most everybody is of similar belief. Yet, if you were to gather a small group of those same people where they felt free to share their thoughts, you'd be amazed. Those same people might have a wide range of opinion of basic things such as creation, virgin birth, grace, sanctity of life. Sometimes my wife or I will hear things and think to ourselves, "Where on earth did you get that opinion? Are you reading the same bible as me?"

Put yourself in the position of an outsider or skeptic. They see us in our little circle arguing over simple issues and this does not even take into account the larger community or world. We swear that our bible is the inerrant word of God and yet, say we are in a group of thirty believers, and fifteen of them brought their bibles to the study, you would probably find several different translations among our group, some of which read quite differently than your own. Do you believe that the Bible is authoritative? What scripture might we go to as a scriptural text for that assumption?

> *"All scripture is God-breathed and is useful for teaching, rebuking, correcting, and training."*
> —2 Timothy 3:16

As I stated before, I will be using scripture as I present my case before you today. I believe it is divinely inspired and I also believe it has been proven to be historically accurate. Listen now as your lawyer tries to present a case and describe the "flavor" of the Early Church.

We find ourselves here in the book of Acts. Jesus has been resurrected from the dead and has risen to heaven just as he said. But before that he even appeared unto many believers. Now we find these disciples were confused and a bit perplexed at all that had happened in their lives and before their eyes.

> *"They all joined together constantly in prayer, along with the women and Mary the mother of Jesus, and with his brothers."*
> —Acts 1:14

> *"In those days Peter stood up among the believers (a group numbering about a hundred and twenty)."*
> —Acts 1:15

Now wait just a minute. So often when people read scripture—if they read it at all—they just rush on to the next verse without giving much thought to it. Maybe they are in a hurry to get their devotional box checked off? I'm teasing. Take a look around you right now. What type of a room are you in? Can you imagine fitting one hundred and twenty people into it? I need to tell you something about me. Before becoming the lawyer here before you today, I was in the construction business. I owned a construction company for about thirty years. During the course of that time I built many homes, additions, and even business spaces. So when I see the above group assembled in Jerusalem, I say to myself . . . "Humm—I wonder, what type of room was that?" That was a good size group of people. Do you suppose that outside of that upper room hung a big "ole" sign that read . . .

First Pentecostal Church of Jerusalem

I doubt it. I don't mean to offend you (much), but many times from now on I will refer to that room or space as a "box." So I, as a builder, wonder what kind of box that must have been?

> *"When the day of Pentecost came, they were all together in one place."*
>
> —Acts 2:1

Rather than just rush on to the next verse, I'm kind of wondering why God gives a hoot about mentioning the **Jewish** Feast of Pentecost. Why is that in my Christian bible? Didn't Jesus come to fulfill or maybe even do away with the Old Testament and usher in a new religion?

That meeting in the upper room got out of control. *God often does His best work when we get—out of control.* The disciples and everybody are amazed at this outpouring—of what? Peter finds himself addressing huge crowds. Evidently this ex-ruffian fisherman was quite powerful!

"Those who accepted his message were baptized, and about three thousand were added to their number that day."
—Acts 2:41

Holy Mackerel!—Is it ok to say that? I wonder if a committee was formed to get right on the planning work. I mean, I was a builder and all, but a building for three thousand? Is that going to be free span or one with supports for the steel bar joists? That's some serious expansion program. What kind of a box are they going to build to hold that kind of crowd?

"Every day they continued to meet together in the Temple courts."
—Acts 2:46

Wait a minute. I thought this was a NEW religion. Jesus himself declared he was giving them a New Covenant. Why are they still meeting in Jewish Temple Courts! Sometimes when I present this information in India or Africa, I like to ask the leaders questions. In India for example, I would ask, "How many of you once were Hindu before becoming a Christian?" Usually at least a third to a half of the pastors will raise their hands. Then I go up to any one in particular and say this: "Sir—how often do you go to the Hindu temple now?" When it dawns upon them, through the translator, what I am saying, it is so fun to see their white eyes open wide against the contrast of their dark brown skin. They shake their head and adamantly say that—no—they no longer go into the temple of that religion! The same is true when I am in Africa and men or women who once were Muslim are posed with the same question. They do not go anywhere near a mosque.

And yet these early Christians are still hanging around the Jewish temple. Curious?

> ". . . And the Lord added to their number daily those who were being saved."
>
> —Acts 2:47

Nothing monumental here, but still more headaches for the *building committee*.

> "One day Peter and John were going up to the temple at the time of prayer."
>
> —Acts 3:1

There they go and do it again . . . going up to that Jewish temple! But hey, you can't hate the results. They come across some crippled guy. They had probably passed him many times before but this time was WAY different. In the name (What's in a NAME?) of Jesus Christ of Nazareth—they command this poor cripple to walk!

> "He jumped to his feet and began to walk. Then he went with them into the temple courts . . ."
>
> —Acts 3:8

You have to give credit where credit is due right? But Peter and John must have blown a perfect opportunity. Weren't they in *the business* of starting a new religion complete with the command to make new disciples? What in the world were they thinking by going into that Jewish temple? That miracle would have been a golden feather in the cap of the First Baptecostal Church of Jerusalem.

"The apostles performed many miraculous signs and wonders among the people. And all the believers used to meet together in Solomon's Colonnade."

—Acts 5:12

Ughh!! Need I elaborate? That was an addition off the side of—you guessed it—the Jewish temple.

Now this next part really gets me. I can understand this band of ignorant and un-churched disciples messing up from time to time, but get a load of what the angel of the Lord himself goes and tells them.

"'. . . Go stand in the temple courts,' he said, 'and tell the people the full message of this new life.' At daybreak they entered the temple courts, as they had been told, and began to teach the people."

—Acts 5:20-21

Am I taking something out of context here? Is God trying to suggest something? The lawyer will continue on and let you decide.

Next we find the apostles, "*. . . rejoicing because they had been counted worthy of* <u>suffering disgrace</u> *for the Name* (What's in a NAME?). *Day after day in the temple courts, and from house to house, they never stopped teaching and proclaiming the good news . . . .*"

(Emphasis mine)   —Acts 5:41-43

May I suggest to you that Jesus never intended to start a new religion? May I also suggest to you that this might be the first mention of a powerful movement? This was a movement that was not contained in big boxes. Rather than that, we are introduced here to a Home Church Movement model. I also want you to pause and ask yourself why it is that God seems to emphasize that word "name" above. It is even capitalized in my bible as well as most others.

> "But Saul began to destroy the church. Going from house to house, he dragged off men and women and put them in prison."
>
> —Acts 8:3

Why is it that this persecutor of the Church and this powerful movement would be going house to house? I suggest to you that this speaks of house churches. He was on a terrible mission and he knew right where to find the offenders. Gatherings of believers were meeting in their homes and yet under some general direction.

> "Saul spent several days with the disciples in Damascus. At once he began to preach in the synagogues that Jesus is the Son of God."
>
> —Acts 9:19-20

Here we find Saul, who has had a personal encounter with the Messiah himself, now filled with the Spirit and purpose. We even know that he was called to the Gentiles, and yet here he goes back into that dusty old tradition and Jewish places of worship. Certainly this would have been another good opportunity for a fresh start.

". . .Barnabas and Saul met with the church and taught great numbers of people. The disciples were called Christians first at Antioch."

—Acts 11:26

I already made a case for what *great numbers* of people consisted of in this exploding movement. And I suggest to you that when they speak of meeting with the church they are not talking about "The Antioch Tour" where they itinerate in as many "boxes" as possible. I believe they were meeting with believers and leaders in House Churches primarily. May I furthermore suggest that this title of Christian was not a big sign of flattery but may rather have been one of mocking? You might look at 1 Peter 4:16.

"On the Sabbath they entered the synagogue and sat down."

—Acts 13:14

Just a little later in Acts 14:1 we find: "At Iconium Paul and Barnabas went as usual into the Jewish synagogue."
Jewish holy day of worship and a Jewish place of worship. Oy Veh!!

"After Paul and Silas came out of prison, they went to Lydia's house, where they met with the brothers and encouraged them."

—Acts 16:40

I wonder if Paul, now no longer referred to as Saul, rejoiced while in prison that he too was worthy to suffer on account of the Name? I suggest to you that Paul and Silas went right on over to Lydia's house and that it was a House Church. Furthermore, I wonder if she is mentioned in this fashion because she was the **leader** of that church. Let this also give credence to the fact that women can be pastors and can be used mightily by the Lord.

> "As his custom was, Paul went into the synagogue, and on three Sabbath days he reasoned with them from the Scriptures . . ."
>
> —Acts 17:2

I include this in my evidence and presentation, but I also want to point something else out. It doesn't have anything to do with the Jewish *flavor* of the Early Church. It is something I like to point out to my listeners since most often I am teaching leaders. I ask them to note the word "reasoned" in the scripture text. I even ask them to underline or circle the word. In my humble opinion, all too often one person—usually a male—stands before a congregation of listeners . . . often times SHOUTS into a microphone, and dominates the teaching for maybe an hour or more—and beats the people into submission with his list of points or continuation of a sermon series. I know that was a long, run-on sentence, but so is the application I speak of. Then the leader sits down and must feel quite satisfied with his delivery and trust that the sheep have all assimilated it. This seems to be the typical church service. I have noticed that in the United States there are often super duper visuals or graphics to accompany said delivery. Overseas, what they lack in visuals, they more than make up for with drama and an ear-bleeding speaker system!

"So he <u>reasoned</u> in the synagogue with the Jews and the God-fearing Greeks."

—Acts 17:17

"Every Sabbath he <u>reasoned</u> in the synagogue, trying to persuade Jews and Greeks."

—Acts 18:4

I'd like to share just a little more as far as reasoning versus lecturing goes. I am sure that in the early church there was often something akin to our preaching style; but I feel many times it was more *organic*. We are told in Corinthians that often a good pattern might be for two or three to share during fellowship, and we are told to <u>test</u> all things. One thing about letting the Spirit lead and others have a part is that it produces results. I find if I allow some discussion and input from the listeners, it is as if some say, "What—really—you actually care what I think?" That in itself brings so much more ownership and energy to our meetings. The second thing is that when you let others participate, they actually learn or absorb the concept and message. You know the axiom, "It's not taught unless it's caught." True leadership and multiplication happens when others catch—and run with the vision.

"Before he sailed, he had his hair cut off at Cenchrea because of a <u>vow</u> he had taken. They arrived at Ephesus, where Paul left Priscilla and Aquilla. He himself went into the synagogue and reasoned with the Jews."

—Acts 18:18-19

Again, here is perhaps the greatest of all apostles or writers in a Jewish worship venue and again—reasoning.

Wait just a minute. Before we scurry on I have a question. Why does God give a hoot that I know about some vow Paul took? I do hope there is something that sheds light on that, unless it was just the style of the day and he was a bit of a hipster.

Since I may have your attention and perhaps you might be one who the Lord can use to spread the gospel, let me make one more comment. We see in the last verse of Acts 18 another powerful orator and ambassador of Christ. Apollos, we are told, "... *vigorously refuted the Jews in public debate, and proved from the Scriptures that Jesus was the Christ.*" I wonder just what passages he found most helpful. Certainly he must have gone to the book of Romans and told them how Jehovah has now reconciled them to himself through salvation in Messiah. Or maybe he elaborated upon how Yeshua is our High Priest taken from the book of Hebrews. And let us not forget about the beautiful Christmas story found in the Gospels. WRONG! Paul and Apollos and other inspired teachers had no difficulty proving from the only writings they had. They spoke from the Torah, the prophets, and all the rest of what we call the Old Testament. I encourage you to broaden your horizons as well and your ability with the whole bible.

> *"Paul entered the synagogue and spoke boldly there for three months, arguing persuasively about the kingdom of God. But some of them became obstinate; they refused to believe and publicly maligned the Way."*
> —Acts 19:8-9

Of course, besides making my point regarding the venue Paul was speaking in, I wonder why God uses that funny term—*the Way?* It is even capitalized in my bible. Is it also in yours? I thought Jesus was here to show us a new way and kind of start a new religion.

And of course that religion is rightly called the Christian religion. We might just touch upon that a bit later. I have it circled in my bible and you might also want to.

> *"But we sailed from Philippi after the Feast of Unleavened Bread . . ."*
>
> —Acts 20:6

I know I'm simple and get stuck on things once in a while, but I wonder why God seems to want me to know about this Feast of Unleavened Bread. It starts immediately after the celebration of Passover. Both are Jewish and I'm not sure what they are doing in the New Covenant part of my bible.

> *"But Paul had decided to sail past Ephesus to avoid spending time in the province of Asia for he was in a hurry to reach Jerusalem, if possible, by the day of Pentecost."*
>
> —Acts 20:16

"Paul, you had a direct encounter with the Lord Jesus. You were commanded to carry the true gospel and entrusted with the revelations others only dreamed about. ENOUGH with celebrating all things Jewish already! And by the way . . . why is your head still shaved?"

You might also note there in Acts 20:20, *"You know that I have not hesitated to preach anything that would be helpful to you but have taught you publicly and from house to house."* I think he is referring to this wonderful new House Church Movement.

Paul and the gang are tremendously effective and we find in verse 20 of Acts 21 where he makes mention of how many thousands of Jews are being converted as well as Gentiles. He says something in verse 24 of the same chapter that has me a bit puzzled though. *"Take these men, join in their purification rites and pay their expenses, so that they can have their heads shaved."* Why does God seem to want me to know this stuff? Is this why Paul himself had his head shaved? And is this still Jewish *funny business?* We see here the famous apostle joining in Nazarite vows. I wonder if Paul even considered himself to be a Christian? We find over in Chapter 24 of Acts that now our friend Paul is on trial before Felix the Roman governor. And what terrible crimes do they accuse of him?

> *"We have found this man to be a troublemaker, stirring up riots among the Jews all over the world. He is a ringleader of the Nazarene sect . . ."*
>
> —Acts 24:5-6

> *". . . I admit that I worship the God of our fathers as a follower of the Way, which they call a sect. I believe with everything that agrees with the Law and that is written in the prophets."*
>
> —Acts 24:14

You have been most patient with me as I have presented this evidence. Our last reference will be taken near the end of the book of Acts. Around verse 23 we find large numbers of people filing in and out of Paul's home where he was teaching them from morning till evening. The exciting book of Acts concludes with this:

> *"For two whole years Paul stayed there in his own rented house and welcomed all who came to see him. Boldly and*

> *without hindrance he preached the kingdom of God and taught about the Lord Jesus Christ."*
> —Acts 28:30-31

I speak often before crowds of church leaders and pastors. Much more often than not, I speak in countries other than the USA. Many times these pastors embrace this evidence I present. It is amazing how they can do so much and be so effective with little means. Their zeal is inspiring. But occasionally, some of them rather wish I would partner with them and help them build a big church and a mighty work. I leave them with this challenge. The greatest apostle of all time, and the one who wrote most of the inspired works of the New Testament, seemed quite content with an outcome most of us would shun. In our upwardly mobile mentality, bigger is better. Larger crowds and bigger budgets and "bigger boxes" must certainly be God's stamp of approval upon **our** ministry. Here we find Paul, shortly before laying down his life for this precious Gospel, ministering out of his very own Home Church. Please think about that.

Well there you have it ladies and gentlemen. I hope I have presented a good case. You have the power to decide if I have twisted scripture to fit my own agenda. I submit to you that the Early Church was powerful and effective. I further submit to you that they embraced and maintained a very Jewish flavor. The Early Church had a very Messianic character and calling.

* Oh Yea . . . *Brain teaser:*

I live in a part of the United States near Niagara Falls. It is actually one of the great wonders of the world. Each year countless people visit from all over the world to take in the sight. What you may not know is that area is also the border between the United States and the nation of Canada. Sometimes people pay to take a helicopter ride to view the majestic falls and of course an international border. You may have not heard the tragic news recently. The pilot lost control and that helicopter went down RIGHT on the border. My question to you is this: in what country did they most likely bury the survivors?

Answers are in the back. . . .

Chapter 3

History
Visit to the Early Church

Thy Kingdom come:

> "Lord—let the kingdom of God begin to dawn on all mankind. Let a worldwide knowledge of God begin to sweep the earth. Establish Your love on the earth, and may the order of everything that is not aligned with your Kingdom purposes change."
> —Dr. Chuck Pierce—Glory of Zion Ministries

We are about to take a trip through history. We will study history and what I present will be after the fashion of a professor. Any good professor researches carefully the material he or she presents. But it is usually given in a lecture fashion and therefore references and credits are assumed and not given. I ask your permission to present in similar fashion. I feel that what I am about to present to you is some of the best, most accurate, and most balanced information I could find. I could, however, paraphrase all of it and pretend it is from my own head and hand. I have no desire to do that. Plus in this day of IPR— Intellectual Property Rights, it is getting harder and harder to **get** credit where credit is due. I have asked for permission from the source to use some of his work in this chapter and I will be happy to give credit. I was delighted with his permission and blessing.

I urge you, if you are interested, to look through the references I give you at the end of my book and check out these sources. I find them to be amazing. You and I were obviously not born at the time of the Early Church. Revisionist historians and "spin-meisters" might have a field day with anything people present no matter if it is absolutely true. You can accept what I present, here as a sort of "Cliff Notes" on some historical events, or in today's terms, "Council of Nicea for Dummies." Just because we were not there to read through the minutes of Church legislative meetings, does not mean it was not monumental.

I asked you early in chapter one, "What do you think of those Jews?" Have you come to any conclusions or opinion? I hope I presented a good case in the last chapter and you are relatively convinced that the Early Church had a Jewish flavor. I think you will find that they just didn't go away after the book of Acts. You may find that the historical record sheds some new light. I highlighted the phrase "Thy **Kingdom** come" at the beginning of this chapter. Let me suggest that when Yahweh either interfaces with a man, or brings a revelation to mankind, something often precedes it. Repentance and the kingdom of God go hand in hand.

We must **repent** for sharing a partial Gospel message.
We have preached a partial, and therefore a false,

gospel. Salvation through the sacrifice of Jesus is only part of the gospel, and serves as our entrance into the Kingdom. The true gospel is the Good News of the Kingdom. This releases the power of God within us to resist the power of the enemy. The power of God is manifested in healing, deliverance, and relationships. The Kingdom has to do with our behavior and discipling people to live by the law of the kingdom (Matthew 5).

We must **repent** of the American mindset of tolerating personal peace and affluence, with Jesus being presented as the means to make us comfortable.

We must **repent** for our failure to perceive and pursue the fullness of the Church. Church is often perceived as a social club or a place to go and "get some of God" once a week. That mentality is wrong. God does not want us to "go to church" in the traditional sense. The question should not be "Where do you go to church?" but "Where are you submitted for training in the work of ministry?"

We must **repent** for abandoning the Jewish responsibilities. God has called us to make Israel jealous. Her re-ingrafting will mean "life from the dead" for Gentiles. We need deeds of love and kindness, intersession and giving to promote her salvation.[6]

—Dan Juster

I mentioned before that I don't know where I am finding you as we continue in this conversation. Perhaps you are a church leader or an involved lay person. Maybe you are a Christian or a follower of the "Way." I do hope that many of you are at least of the assumption that you are *spiritual* even if you do not belong to any particular church or denomination. And by all means, if you are fed up to the eyeballs with religion of any flavor or fashion, I sincerely hope we can continue to talk. No matter if you're an outsider or insider, whether you're a participant or spectator, or even card carrying skeptic, I believe you have an opinion and observation of both religion and church. In your observation, does the church "work?" Has there ever been a time when it actually resembled the body of our Savior on earth with Him as the head? As I present this professorial lecture for the next few minutes, I will be drawing from an excellent book called *Messianic Church Arising* by Dr. Robert Heidler.

Do you think you have come upon this by accident, or does it resonate so far with something deep within you? Is it possible that many of us have been looking for something we didn't quite know how to describe? Have our life experiences, both positive and painful, brought us to a place where we can entertain a different view of church, religion, and relationship? Could this be a stepping stone toward a **return to innocence**? Dr. Heidler states that this church has often been called the *early church*, the *New Testament Church*, or the *first-century* church. He likes to refer to it as the Messianic Church. It's the church that would work in any generation. "It is the church as God designed it." Let's let him guide us through this lecture for the next few minutes.

> *The early church was the most powerful institution the world had ever seen. It exploded onto the world stage in Acts chapter two, and nothing had the power to stand against it. Pagan religions could not compete with it. Greek philosophy could not comprehend it. Persecution only purified it and made it grow more rapidly.*

On the day of Pentecost, the Holy Spirit fell on 120 people in the city of Jerusalem. By the end of that DAY, the infant church had grown to about 3000 members (Acts 2).

Within about a year, the church more than tripled in size, numbering more than ten thousand people. Some historians estimate that by the time of Stephan's martyrdom (as early as two years later) the church in Jerusalem had grown to about 20,000 members.

A good example of the enormous explosion in this movement is seen in the church at Ephesus. Acts 19 indicates that Paul went to Ephesus, started a church, and remained there for two years teaching his converts. During those two years, not only was the entire city of Ephesus evangelized (a city of around 200,000 people), but all of the cities in the surrounding province were also reached. The churches in Colossae, as well as the seven churches mentioned in Revelation 2 and 3, were all probably planted during that two year period.

By the time Paul wrote his first letter to Timothy around A. D. 63, the church in Ephesus had probably grown to around sixty thousand members. No wonder Timothy felt intimidated when Paul installed him as the leader of that congregation! At its height, the church in Ephesus may have had as many as 100,000 members.

In the year A. D. 112, about eighty years after Pentecost, the Roman author Pliny wrote a letter to Emperor Trajan. In this letter, he complained that in the province of Asia Minor, where Ephesus was, ". . . temples to the (pagan)

gods are almost totally forsaken and Christians are everywhere a multitude."

This pattern was repeated throughout the empire.
Tertullian writes to the pagans in his Apologia, "We
have filled every place belonging to you—cities, islands,
castles, towers, assemblies, your very camp, your tribes,
companies, palace, senate, and forum! We leave you your
temples only, We can count your armies; our numbers in
a single province will be greater."

According to Chrysostrom, the Christian population of
Antioch in his day was about 100,000, or one half of
the whole city.

Perpetual Revival:

The early church experienced what no other brand of
Christianity has ever been able to reproduce: a perpetual
revival lasting hundreds of years. A sustained—multi-
generational revival! It spread everywhere; and the world
could not stand against it.

By the end of the first century, the early church had spread
throughout the known world. It extended from India on the
East to England on the West, and from Germany on the
North to Ethiopia on the South. Its expansion amazed the
world. In one city, when Paul and Silas came to town, the
pagans cried out in horror, "These men who have turned
the world upside down have come here also" (Acts 17:6).

It was not unusual for a church to be planted in a city
and rapidly grow from 20 to 30,000 members. Some

historians estimate that by the end of the third century, half of the population of the Roman Empire had converted to Christianity. This growth took place within a totally pagan, immoral culture, during times of severe persecution.

The historian Philip Schaff writes, "It may be fairly asserted that about the end of the third century the name of Christ was known, revered, and persecuted in every province and every city of the empire," and, "In all probability at the close of the third century the church numbered ten million souls."

A Visit to the Early Church:

The early church operated primarily on two levels: the house church and the congregation. Even if the church grew to 20 or 30,000 members, its primary unit would still be the house church. From time to time the house churches would also congregate in a larger group (the congregation). This often took place outdoors or in a rented auditorium. In Jerusalem, they met in the temple courts.

Saturday Evening

Most church services would begin with the people getting in a ring (or several concentric rings) and dancing Jewish-style ring dances (like the Hora).

Clement of Alexandria (writing in the third century) describes the "daughters of God" leading the church in a ring dance: "The righteous are the dancers; the music is a song of the King of the Universe. The maidens strike the lyre, the angels praise, the prophets speak; the sound

33

of music issues forth, they run and pursue the jubilant band; those that are called make haste, eagerly desiring to receive the Father."

Ambrose of Milan, the man who led Augustine to the lord, writing in A. D. 390 exhorted his people to worship with these words: "Let us dance as David did. Let us not be ashamed to show adoration to God. Dance bound up with faith is a testimony to the living grace of God. He who dances as David danced, dances with grace."

St. Basil (4th Century) wrote, "Could there be anything more blessed than to imitate on earth the ring dance of the angels."

Much dancing—Great fellowship—and a meal—Love (Agape) feast.

Those who have studied revival literature recall that a 'tangible sense of God's Presence' has frequently accompanied the great revivals of history. The 'manifest Presence of God' is in fact, the hallmark of true revival. In the presence of a holy God, sinners find salvation, backsliders find repentance, and the miraculous becomes commonplace.

Oftentimes there would be—great worship . . . Testimony . . . Words of knowledge . . . Scripture reading and explanation . . . Prophecy . . . Miracles.

Iranaeus (writing around A. D. 195) tells us that in his day, prophetic words, tongues, and miracles of healing were common in the church. He adds that the church frequently saw people raised from the dead through the prayers of the saints!

How would you like to be a part of a church like that? That's what the early church was. It was a temple where the glory of God dwelt. On any given Saturday evening there would have been hundreds of such meetings all over a city like Rome or Ephesus and elsewhere.

*Many believe that now is the time—the **appointed time**, the **Kairos** time—chosen by God for the **restoration** of His church.*

The Death of the Early Church:

The early church was the most powerful institution the world had ever seen. Pagan religions could not compete with it. Greek philosophy could not comprehend it and persecution only purified it and caused it to grow. Yet by the sixth century, it was largely destroyed. By the year 600, almost nothing that had characterized the early church remained. The church became a corrupt political power, hated and feared by the common people, with little evidence of the life and power it had once known.

How did the Messianic Church die?

The "death knell" for the early church was the "conversion" of the Roman emperor Constantine.

Constantine, alarmed by rumors that the throne might be lost . . . panicked. He was challenged to battle by rival Maxentius. Constantine prayed to his "supreme god" for help. To Constantine, the supreme god was Mithras—the Persian sun god. He reportedly saw a vision of a flaming cross in the sky next to the sun, along

35

with the words "Conquer by this." He fought and won the battle.

His next move was to declare from the throne that he was a follower of Jesus. The Christians could hardly believe it. They had gone through centuries of scattered local persecution. Thousands had been tortured and murdered. Sacred writings had been confiscated and leadership often killed. But now a new Roman Emperor had come to the throne claiming to be a follower of Jesus.

Not only had Constantine made Christianity the favored religion, he tried to **improve** it.

In return for his favor, Constantine demanded control. One of the titles given to a Roman emperor was "pontifex maximus" (high priest). By Roman law, the emperor was in charge of all religious affairs in the empire. The emperor, for centuries, had been head of the pagan religious system.

In the year 325, Constantine called and presided over the first general council of the church, the Council of Nicea.

Now that Christianity was legal, Christians warmly accepted Constantine as Pontifex Maximus of the church! They hailed him as a new apostle. In his "Church of the Holy Apostles," Constantine set up monuments for 13 people: the 12 apostles and **himself!** And his monument was bigger than the others.

1. The Death of the House Church

Constantine viewed the early Christians as rather primitive and unsophisticated. They seemed to lack the

*organizational skill of the Romans. Remember—for
centuries—the backbone of the early church was the
House Church.*

*Shortly after he legalized Christianity, Constantine built
a church called St. John Lateran in Rome. The style of
this building is called a **basilica**. Its **interior design
was patterned after the Imperial Throne Room of
the palace!***

*Encouraged and financed by the imperial government,
this pattern for church construction spread rapidly.
Basilica-type churches were built all over the empire!
A Roman **basilica** was a large hall built for meetings,
business and law. At one end was a semi-circular part
where the judges sat. The building usually had two rows
of columns, which made a high central part and a lower
aisle on either side. The light came in from windows
above the columns. As the Roman Empire spread, every
city had a basilica.*

*Does the following illustration look at all familiar to
churches you have been in?[7]*

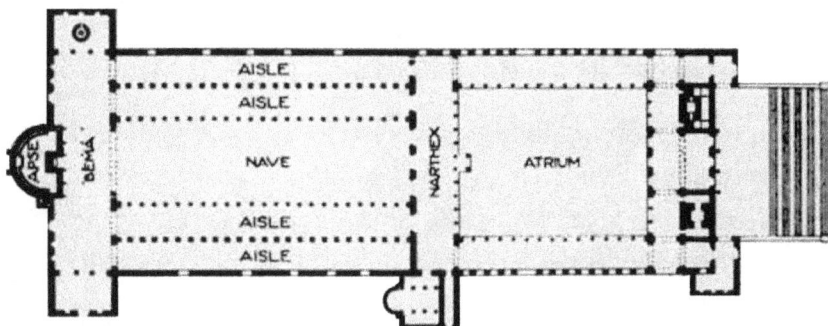

Constantine then enacted a law that "houses of prayer" must be abolished, forbidding Christians from holding church in private homes. This decree was harshly worded and designed to "strike terror into the minds of his subjects." It went on to prohibit "holding church any place but the Catholic Church."

2. A Change in Worship

Less than one year after his "conversion" Constantine made the following decree: "I am going to make plain to them what kind of worship is to be offered to God."

Worship in the house church had been Spirit led and intimate, with little in the way of set forms and liturgies. In Constantine's Roman mind, the highest expression of worship was found in the solemn rituals of the Roman Imperial Court. He cut the church off from its Jewish roots and grafted it into the root of Greek paganism.

3. Rejection of the Church's Jewish Roots

Around the large metropolitan cities of Rome and Alexandria, the church had been strongly influenced by paganism and Greek philosophy. These churches rejected much of their Jewish heritage, mingling pagan practices and ideas with those of the bible.

Across most of the empire, however, the church still held fast to the Jewish heritage received from the apostles. Most continued to celebrate Sabbaths and feasts, stressed the learning of Torah, and continued in their rich covenant heritage.

Constantine's attempt to purge the church of its Jewish elements began with the Council of Nicea (A. D. 325). In the letter of Constantine to the bishops following the council, he declared that it was improper for a church to follow the customs of the Jews. Speaking of the church's observance of Passover, he wrote, "Let us, then, have nothing in common with the Jews, who are our adversaries . . . the murderers of our Lord."

4. The Influx of Paganism

Constantine claimed to be Christian, but did not seem to understand who Jesus was. He continued to also be a devout follower of Mithras the Persian sun god. He may have thought that Jesus was a manifestation of Mithras and equated the cross symbol to him. It had been used for centuries before with **no association to Jesus and was not used by the early church believers.**

In 321, when Constantine made the Christian day of worship a Roman holiday, he didn't call it "Christ Day." He called it "the venerable day of the Sun." (That is where we get the name Sunday). Interesting—the so called Christian emperor Constantine named the Christian day of worship in honor of the pagan sun god!

Before the time of Constantine, Christians never celebrated Christ's birthday. But pagan Romans had long celebrated December 25 as the birthday of Mithras. Also known as Saturnalia, Mithras' birthday was one of the Romans' favorite festivals, a time for good cheer and gift giving. On that one day of the year, masters would serve their slaves.

Romans would give food to the children of the poor. How does it come that Jesus was viewed as a manifestation of the Sun god, and Saturnalia was declared a Christian holiday . . . "Christmas, the birthday of Jesus."

Another new feast for the church was the celebration of the spring fertility festival. Each year the pagans held a feast to honor the goddess of fertility. The Canaanites called this goddess Asherah. Persians called her Aestarte. Babylonians called her Ishtar. The ancient Britons called her Eastre (from which we get the word estrogen).

It bothered Constantine that Christians celebrated Christ's death and resurrection on Passover, a Jewish holiday. At Nicea, he outlawed this celebration and directed that Christ's death and resurrection be celebrated on the Sunday following the first full moon after the vernal equinox, a time associated with the spring fertility festival.

Perhaps the strangest part of this twist from biblical context and truth is that, in the English-speaking world, we did not even change the name. Easter Sunday. Some forward thinking Christians now call it Resurrection Sunday . . . Still at the wrong time of the year . . . On the wrong day . . . and often we still like to placate the kiddos with Fertility goddess egg hunts.

By the end of the fourth century, the empire was officially "Christianized." Pagan temples became Christian churches. Pagan shrines became Christian shrines. Very confusing! One common cult was the cult of Isis. Isis, an Egyptian goddess, was called the Great Virgin" and "The Mother of God." She is commonly shown holding the child Horus, *in a pose very similar to the early Romanized Christian pictures of Mary and Jesus.*

By the year 800, church councils had outlawed Jewish lifestyle once embraced by Jesus and the apostles. For a Christian to observe the Sabbath or celebrate Passover became a crime punishable by death. Obedience to these decrees was enforced through torture and execution.[8]

Well I don't know about you, but I am certainly glad to have had Dr. Heidler as our guest lecturer for this section of our study. I know for me, when I first discovered the information he shared with us, my eyes were wide open. I began to look at scripture and especially tradition in such a different light. It was like all of a sudden I had to examine so many things I had been taught and just assumed was right and proper.

You might want to refer back to the picture a short while ago. It was the floor plan of a typical basilica. Did you notice the raised platform at one end? That is called the *aspe*, which was reserved for the clergy. I guess the Bishop and his advisors sat there. That throne is designed to reflect the Bishop's authority. Facing the *aspe* was a large open area. There might often be support columns in that area. This is where the Bishop's subjects (members of the church) would come and listen. I don't know about you, but now that I have become aware, I have noticed this style and pattern in every country and almost every church I have ever been in.

Have you ever wondered why we sit the way we do in our churches? Why do we just assume that we are to stare at the back of the heads of those in front of us? Why are we much like herd animals as we often seek out our similar "feeding place" in our meetings each week? You may think I am making too much out of this, but I disagree. As I consider this, I look to not just small fellowship meetings or home churches, but I also look to scripture in Revelation that speaks about how we will all be gathering *around* the throne in heaven. Revelation 4 gives us a beautiful description of worship in heaven. The elders, the angels, and the multitudes all appear to be *encircled around* the throne and worship the Lamb.

I will never forget being escorted in as the guest speaker in a church in India. It was a small rectangular building made up of bricks where many had fallen out. The roof was thatched with simple pole rafters. The floor was mostly a dirt and concrete mixture. My heart was so saddened when I entered and beheld the ceremony. I, of course, was ushered across the room where there were a few chairs waiting for me to join the other pastors in attendance. Believe it or not, but in this rickety church there was a platform made in the floor. A two to three inch rise in the simple floor announced that this is where the "bishop" should sit. In India, men and women most commonly sit on the floor in many of the meetings at which I speak. How sad it seemed to me to see these beautiful people sitting cross-legged on the floor while I was given the seat of honor with great fanfare, fresh water, and a flower garland to wear around my neck. Well—I don't play very nicely, and as I said, don't mind shaking things up a bit. I told them I would not proceed until we all formed a circle. We passed out as many plastic chairs as we had. I asked these humble people to please sit along with us and in between pastor or leader alike. They looked at me incredulous, as if to say, "We don't dare . . . we have NEVER been offered such an opportunity." The common people loved it that day, as well as leaders who had humble hearts. Some of the others leaders endured it, but were plainly ruffled. I actually "reasoned" with them that day and we had a wonderful discussion instead of me taking the microphone (yes microphone—on steroids—in that dinky building) and blaring at them for an hour.

Dr. Heidler told us several things about Jewish customs that you may have never known. Sometimes I get myself in trouble when I teach and mention some of those facts. I don't know what time of year you happen to be reading my book. But can you recall, often around Christmas each year, a big hoopla seems to make the news or at least a buzz in Christian circles. "Don't you dare try to make me say **Happy Holidays!** It's Christmas . . . . This is a Christian nation . . . If you don't like it—why don't you just pack up and leave? . . . Stinking politically correct people anyway!" Does that ring any bells? Sometimes I gently pose the following question, and I think I will ask you the same. I'm not asking your opinion of the current president, but do you think that at some times in our nation's history there have been wonderful statesmen? Do you think our nation was at least, at one time, a Christian nation, founded on solid Christian principles and tradition? Would it surprise you to know that not until around 1830 was Christmas practiced in America? Did you know, that at one time there was legislation on record in some States that Christmas was not to be celebrated, and that our "founding fathers" did not celebrate it? And of course the early followers of the WAY . . . the sect of the Nazarene . . . whom you call Christians . . . did not celebrate Christmas. I'm not trying to ruin your day or declare that you stop making Merry. Each of us is admonished to follow Scripture and the leading of the Holy Spirit.

There is more that can be said, but let me bring up one more little subject. I encourage you to ask yourself if the cross is the true symbol of our faith. And before you get mad at me for daring to mention it, let me give you an example of how much I used to love that symbol. I told you in a previous chapter that I was a builder for many years. I also have been a follower of Yeshua for most of my life. If you had asked me to build you a house or even remodel a bathroom, let me tell you a little secret. Someplace, maybe in the wet cement of the foundation, or way on top a chimney, or somewhere behind the access panel to a shower or behind the kitchen cabinets, I left a mark. I would often draw three crosses with the center one being the most prominent. It was just my little way of honoring my Savior and perhaps letting some later person know that a Christian did their work. It was a way of honoring Yeshua. So I assure you, I loved the symbol of the cross. But then somebody has to go mess with my head (theology) and tell me that it really was not a Christian symbol.

Did you know that the cross was one of the most barbaric forms of death and torture the Romans preferred to use? You just don't get "kind of" crucified. It is a death sentence. Do you remember when criminals in the United States were sometimes executed by electricity? They even had a nickname for the device called the electric chair: "Ole Sparky." It has to be about one of the most barbaric forms of execution the American empire has invented or used. Hanging was far more merciful. What if Yeshua had been sentenced to die in an electric chair? Do you think for a minute you would wear a little gold electric chair around your neck? I doubt if I would have formed that image in the wet cement. I don't know what country you are in as you read this, but I bet in the following there are some similarities. I find that in my country all sorts of people wear a cross or crosses. Some have them tattooed upon their bodies. Hollywood stars wear them—gang bangers—pimps and players—religious people of all denominations, as well as good hearted folks that simply want to honor their Lord and Savior Yeshua.

I just ask you to think upon these things. I told you that I serve in several nations. Sometimes I ask people to be careful. Do you think that the Muslim people in your country see that cross and think warm or convicting thoughts about how Yeshua died for them? Do you think when my African friend sees that lovely cross against my white skin he or she wants to hear more about salvation? No . . . For many, many people in the world, the cross represents superiority, arrogance, Crusades or Colonialism. The people are not blind, and in every country I have been in, the cross is worn by a wide spectrum of people. Remember, it was not used by the early church. It has been used for centuries by pagan religions. When we are told to "carry our cross," are we encouraged to flash our bling like a Hollywood star or punk . . . or to consider ourselves dead to this world and dead to our own ambitions? Let us please just be open to examining our beliefs and practices in light of Scripture and the Holy Spirit.

Oh, by the way, did I further get under your skin by referring to Jesus as Yeshua during these paragraphs about the cross? We have become so accustomed to using his nickname Jesus. Remember there was no letter "J" . . . in neither Greek nor Hebrew, at the time our Savior walked the earth. Don't worry; I am not trying to bind you to legalism, as some who have discovered the truths I have listed above. Some are embracing our return to our Jewish roots so vehemently that the pendulum has swung out of balance. I believe I was born again many years ago and I was saved in Jesus' name. I invited Jesus into my heart and life and he did not cross his arms and say, "Not till you get my name right, Junior."

You may get the impression that I am one angry fellow . . . that I have lost the joy of my salvation. Let me state that I realize I only stand here in the grace of God and upon free ground that pioneers in the faith have won for me. I wrestle with our traditions and customs. Each of us has to account for our own revelation and convictions. One thing that stands out to me when I ponder all of this, is how **merciful** and **gracious** is our God. He loves us. The bible says that "we see through a glass darkly." We have our own lenses on of tradition and apathy. Is it not amazing that Yahweh sent his Son to give his life for us while we were still sinners? He comes to us even when we are so blind we name sacred times after pagan gods! We have such compromise and mixture and yet he draws us into truth and relationship with him. He loves his church in the same manner as he loves me: broken . . . stubborn . . . in need of transformation and redemption.

🦆 🦆 🦆

Brain teaser:

One thing I really love to do is scuba dive. For that matter, I just love being near the ocean. Oh man, to be out on a boat, riding the waves with the wind and sea splash, to feel the sun on my skin—now that's a good day. I noticed another boat in the harbor as we were getting ready to go out to sea. It had a ladder over the side like most boats do. It looked like an aluminum ladder with rungs one foot apart. This boat had what appeared to be a 10-foot ladder and the water came up to the second rung. The tide comes in at the rate of one-half foot per hour in that coastal area. My question is this: how many hours will it take for the water to **touch** the fifth rung?

Answers in back ☺

Chapter 4

HIS Church

We now enter the third part of what I often use in seminar fashion when teaching this material. I have presented a case as a lawyer in regards to what the Early Church looked like. Then I took us through a glimpse of history as perhaps a professor might. Now I come to you as a friend. Although by this time, some may be quite sure they aren't going to "friend" me any time soon. I know it can be hard to look at our traditions or examine our own motives. I realize this and therefore, whenever I can, I start out this section with something that ALWAYS lightens the mood and can be a whole lot of fun.

To begin with though, I need to frame something with just another trip back into history. Do you remember ever hearing the phrase "the sun never sets upon the British Empire?" I remember it and have seen the quote more than once in my studies. Do you know what it means? It means that at one point in history the British Empire controlled so much land, nations and people groups that, as the world turned under the sun, there would always be daylight cast upon at least one area of their dominion.

I have mentioned several times that I minister in other countries. I remember even out loud praying a few years ago that Yahweh would specifically give me a message and that He would make me a messenger. I find it interesting that each of the countries where he seems to have called me have something in common. It does not matter if I am in India, or Ghana, or the island nation of Jamaica, or here in the United States; each, at one time or another, was under the rule or governance of the British Empire. Each has been under their influence and might.

I think we are all glad that we have thrown off their sovereignty. I think we each might admit that they indeed had pretty effective forms of governance as well as engineering, but we weren't especially thrilled with their system of control. Do you remember how they ruled? They ruled with what is termed an **iron fist.** They quickly would put down rebellion or resistance and often times they were brutal. Indeed, for almost three hundred years they were the leader of the world and for a couple centuries at least, the most powerful nation on earth. The Union Jack was feared and revered. Hey, do you remember how they often fought? They were so bold that they would take line after line of soldiers . . . stand them in broad daylight . . . not even behind cover of trees or tanks, and completely dominate the opposition. I hope you are picturing this in your own mind as I write. Can you picture the main weapon they used in battles such as this? It was a long rifle. It only fired one single shot at a time. Each brave (or conscripted) troop would stand in his place along that line. They would wait until the enemy got within range and then fire their round. With rifle smoke in the air and steel balls whizzing past, they would stand or kneel—mind you, kneel—while a soldier behind them took aim and fired. During this time they would frantically dig into their supplies and reload. They didn't just jam another 30 shot clip of 223 caliber bullets into their machine gun. No sir! They would take out their black powder canister and put some into the barrel of the gun, then place a ball down the shaft, and then tamp down the wadding. Then, if they had not been run over by the enemy or shot themselves, they would take aim and fire. Can you even imagine?

https://www.google.com/search?q=british+battle+formation+pictures&rlz

Because I love a good visual aid in my speaking, I made two British long rifles of my own in my shop. Alas, because TSA isn't a big fan of 48-inch guns going through an international customs check, I made two-piece toy ones out of wood. They really are quite slick though: Two-piece guns with two holes in the center of each, where I use golf tees to keep them steady when assembled. They fit nicely in my suitcase and so far have not been confiscated! When I do this demonstration in other countries, the curiosity immediately builds as those in attendance see me uncover the guns near the stage. They do look quite realistic. By this time I have given them the entire history lesson you read above about the British Empire. It is time to have us a little fun.

Are any of you hunters? Have any of you, man or woman, ever fired a gun? Here in the US I have no problem getting numerous hands raised in the air. Overseas, however, governments have been a little more repressive and certainly most people do not have the economic means. To have something so far down on the list as a gun—or five—is beyond their life experience. I always manage to find a few in the crowd though, who may have been a soldier or policeman. I have the audience give a big round of applause when I find two with enough courage to come to the stage and participate in a little demonstration. In front of their peers, I give them a brief but thorough training in my best British accent. They will be asked to simply take their toy gun—aim it at the back of the room—shout "BOOM"—then kneel—pull out the two golf tees—pull the stock away from the barrel and back again—put back the tees—stand and fire. Simple, right? Do you think you could do it? Surely this is not nearly as difficult as loading black powder, coupled with the horrors of real war.

They have now been conscripted into the Royal British Army. I explain to them that soon they will be off to battle, that the enemy is going to come barging through those rear doors of the meeting. I ask them if they have any questions. I explain that I know this might be new to them and I (of course) do not want to embarrass them in front of their peers. So for that reason I explain we will only be firing three shots in today's *war*. I place one soldier kneeling and one standing behind, and give them a proper salute! "Oh," I explain. "One more thing I must mention. The year is not 1820—but it is now indeed 2016." Now mind you,

I am speaking in a microphone, and I already told you that in Third World countries the amplification is on steroids.

"Here they come. Steady on chap. FIRE! FIRE I say. Come on, shoot. Kneel down now. Sir . . . quickly . . . reload your weapon . . . You, man—FIRE . . . Faster . . . FIRE or we'll all be dead. Reload! Reload!"

Well, we go through this shouting and simulated war with great drama and fun. It is so comical to see them fumbling with the golf tees as they reassemble their weapons (simulating the reloading process). The others in attendance are usually laughing like mad during all this and many have their camera phones out recording the skirmish. The drama builds as they do their best and I keep shouting orders and instructions. Then I take the microphone cupped in my hands and blare out staccato sounds that everyone knows announce AK-47s are being fired. Everybody knows what this sound represents, even in countries where very few own or have fired weapons.

"Oh," I say. "We've been overrun. Our audience is dead. There is blood everywhere! You're buddy is wounded. No more boom. No more boom."

As I collect the toy guns and my soldiers go back to their seats, we do a debriefing. "What happened?" I ask. "Why is there so much blood?" I even heard one of the soldiers declare, "But Sir, this is how I was trained. In fact, this is how my father and grandfather were trained in the British military." Does it really matter how well you are trained or how zealous you are in a situation like we just saw?

The point is this: times change and we must change with them. What may have been effective for decades or even centuries, has gone by the wayside. In fact, only a fool would dare to wage a war with antiquated methods that are as ineffective as my toy wooden guns. You only need to look at how life has changed around you in so many fields.

We have been talking about the Church in some of this book. How do you think we are doing as a church as a collective unit? Are we changing with the times? How are we doing as far as changing or affecting our societies? Perhaps you're not a Christian or follower of *The Way*, or not a member of any church. What is your opinion of "the Church?" Do you think the Christian church is effective in your country or changing the society you live in? I mentioned that martial arts motto, "evolve or become irrelevant." Are we evolving and if so, is that toward compromise or is it toward purity and becoming the *real deal*?

Let me give you the following anecdote. A couple years ago I was speaking before a church audience. I had recently found out that there are an alarming number of churches closing down across this state and even across the country. Furthermore, according to what I studied, on any given "worship weekend" there were only about 15% of the population in what we would call a house of worship. That means on most any given Friday, Saturday, or Sunday, only about 15% of people are in a church setting which leaves 85% not involved. Some are absent for a number of reasons. Some cannot get out to services due to their age or transportation issues. Some have been "church hurt" and their offense keeps them at a distance. But most just don't give a hoot. It is just not something that draws them, or that they care to make the effort for, during their scheduled list of things to do. Most do not feel the benefit outweighs the effort—or risk!

I asked a Christian friend of mine if he could do a little bit of research for me. He works for one of the biggest mobile phone providers in the US. I asked him if he knew how many people in our general area, both city and rural, used mobile phones. He said he wasn't sure right then but it would be easy to find that out. It is common demographic information. About two weeks later he came back to me and said that according to their studies, around 85% of all the people in this area had mobile phones. I thought to myself how interesting was that report. Eighty-five percent of people have cell phones and yet I can bet you my friend hears a certain theme during his management meetings. They are not happy with reaching 85%. They want that number up in the nineties—and preferably on their towers and devices! There is no way they will just sit compliantly and figure that people know where their store is without a good reason to come in. Cell phone companies don't believe people are just lazy, and they don't try to make them feel guilty for not having a cell phone! Is there a cellular phone Hell where the 15% will surely end up if they don't clean up their act?

Do you think there are any causes for some of what I mentioned above?

Tradition:

~ Noun   1. The handing down of statements, beliefs, legends, customs, information, etc. from generation to generation, especially by word of mouth or practice.

          2. (in theology)

             a. Among Jews—a body of laws and doctrines, or any one of them, held to have been received from Moses and originally handed down orally from generation to generation.

             b. Among Christians—a body of teachings, or any one of them, held to have been delivered by Christ and His apostles but not committed to writing.

Many times when I am presenting in person, I like to shake things up a little. Instead of standing on some elevated platform, I much prefer walking near, or being closer to, my listeners. Sometimes I hold up a couple of pictures or stroll through the isle so that all may see. I do have to be very careful because some governments feel a picture or two of mine are offensive. If they only knew that in no way is my intent to mock or ridicule. For example, I tell them that there is an expression in my country that speaks of "stepping on toes." You probably all know that what I mean by "stepping on your toes" is that I perhaps may say something that offends you or hits a little too close to home. We Americans also have a saying that goes like, "If the shoe fits—wear it." Now in India or Africa it is most often the custom to take off my sandals or shoes and leave them at the door along with even hundreds of others. I tell them that of all the sandals lined up there, only one pair fits these big "ole" white feet. So this expression in the context of what I present to you is this: hopefully, if I say something here that is indeed true of you or how you think—please accept it as your own and do not deny that it doesn't "fit" you.

Sometimes I walk among the people and show a picture of an idol—a statue of one of that country's religious gods. When I show this same picture in the United States, some people act almost smug. Like, "Oh my word Henry, can you believe how backward those people are?" I might even mention that in India, for example, there are animals sometimes referred to as "Sacred Cows." Oftentimes they are adorned with flowers and such and allowed to wander the streets or brought on parade at certain festival times. India is such a beautiful and diverse country. They, more than many peoples, have been viewed with disdain for their religious practices and views. Several times I have come back from an overseas trip and I have asked God to show me what idols we have in our own land, and show me the traditions that we hold dear to our national identity and religious beliefs. I want to declare to you that people in all countries have their own *Sacred Cows*. Every religion and people group have traditions that are sacred and they do not like them to be diminished or belittled. We as a people all pretty much dislike and avoid change. So all that to say this: I may step on a few toes in the following pages. I mean no offense, and please do not feel you have to change even a little bit on my account.

I hope you enjoyed the previous pictures. Are they idols or simply magnificent creations of art? Each country takes great pride in them, and multiple thousands of travelers visit each yearly. All of them are about the size of "Lady Liberty" and some are much larger. And speaking of Lady Liberty, why a statue of a woman . . . erected at a time when women were not even allowed to vote? How are your toes? ☺

The Danger of the Traditions of Men

He answered and said unto them, "Well has Esaias prophesied of you hypocrites, as it is written, 'This people honors me with their lips, but their heart is far from me. Howbeit in vain do they worship me, teaching for

doctrines the commandments of men.' For laying aside
the commandment of God, you hold the tradition of men,
as the washing of pots and cups: and many other such
like things you do." And he said unto them, "Full well
you reject the commandment of God, that you may keep
your own tradition."

—Mark 7:6-9 (See also Matt 15:7-9)

It's no secret that many "Christian" churches have
become abusive businesses disguised as churches
run by CEOs disguised as shepherds. Churches like
this prey on the vulnerable and unwary and cater
to human selfishness in order to attract and recruit
members. Those in the world can usually see this
far easier than most Christians who are usually too
close to the problem to recognize it. Sad to say, many
people have turned away from faith in Jesus Christ
and want nothing more to do with Christianity
in general because of the pain and suffering that
they have endured at the hands of these so-called
"churches" and their counterfeit leaders. Jesus gets
blamed for the folly of rebellious men (and women)
who refuse to adhere to the clear teachings of the
Bible. Instead, these false leaders teach their own
ideas, theories and opinions as if they were the truth
and the clear commands of Christ.

As noted above, the Bible says in Mark 7:6-7, "*This people
honors me with their lips, but their heart is far from me. Howbeit in
vain do they worship me, teaching for doctrines the commandments
of men.*"

Why then do so many professing Christians embrace the commandments of men as if they were actually the doctrines of Christ? In verse 9, Jesus gives us the answer, *"Full well you reject the commandment of God, that you may keep your own tradition."*

The reason that so many professing Christians embrace the false teachings of so many powerful "churchmen" is so that they can keep the traditions that they have grown so fond of and have come to love so much. But Jesus made it very clear that man-made traditions are very dangerous. We read in Mark 7 verse 13, *"Making the Word of God of none effect through your tradition, which you have delivered [handed down]: and many such like things you do."*

Since the traditions of men make the Word of God of none effect, this makes the traditions of men one of the most, if not the most, dangerous enemies of the Christian faith. The following verses demonstrate why. I did not include verses 10–12 above in the King James translation because in most translations these verses are difficult to understand, but the Amplified translation sheds some light:

> *"For Moses said, 'Honor (revere with tenderness of feeling and deference) your father and your mother,' and, 'He who curses or reviles or speaks evil of or abuses or treats improperly his father or mother, let him surely die.' But [as for you] you say, 'A man is exempt if he tells [his] father or [his] mother, What you would otherwise have gained from me [everything I have that would have been of use to you] is Corban, that is, is a gift' [already given as an offering to God], Then you no longer are permitting him to do anything for [his] father or mother [but are letting him off from helping them]. Thus you are nullifying and*

making void and of no effect [the authority of] the Word of God through your tradition, which you [in turn] hand on. And many things of this kind you are doing."
—Mark 7:10-13 (AMP)

In context, we see here that the traditions of men spoken of in the previous passage of Scripture are referring to the practices of the Pharisees who chose to teach their manmade traditions instead of teaching simple obedience to God's Word in the area of the care owed by children to their aging fathers and mothers. The Pharisees taught that a man was exempt from his obligation to financially help his father and mother if he already gave money to the temple treasury (Corban). Jesus said at the end of verse 13 that there were other similar things that they were doing.

It is no mystery how the Word of God is actually nullified and made of none effect. Obviously we see here that what causes this monumental problem is man's word being taught and observed instead of God's Word being taught and obeyed. Today we see this problem on an epidemic level. Christians are regularly instructed to obey the complex and confusing teachings of men rather than the clear and obvious teachings of the Bible. Most commands in the Word of God are so simple that even a child can understand them. Yet counterfeit leaders pull off their con rather effectively by convincing their followers that their typically complicated teachings (of men) are actually the teachings of the Bible when in fact they are not. They do this by twisting Scriptures and lifting verses out of context in order to make theses verses look like they are saying something that the Bible does not say.

I want to briefly mention here that many Christians who follow the traditions of men rather than the ways of Christ, have no clue that their worship of God (e.g. Sunday morning service) is therefore done in vain. Ironically and hypocritically, they sing songs of worship to God while they give their allegiance and obedience to men and to their false teachings.[9]

—Paul Howey

I think what Paul Howey said above is relevant and I include it rather than piece together a few quotes from him. While I'm at it, may I give you another reading I found?

GOD HATES RELIGION

God Hates Religion

Yes, God hates religion . . .

I will give you Biblical support for that statement in a moment.

Someone may be thinking, "I thought God invented religion!" Sorry, but God invented Man, and Man invented religion.

Humankind is, by our very nature, (designed so by our Creator), drawn to relationships: relationships that range from familial, to friendships, to marital as well as communal. These relationships that we don't even think about give us insight into what God intended for us. From the time we are born we learn that the family relationship provides security and safety and unconditional love. (That is why we call God the "Father.") A healthy family creates a relationship of trust, security and encouragement. As we grow older we learn the value of a loyal friend that we can trust with our cares and to stand beside us when we need help. (Jesus is referred to as the "friend that sticks closer than a brother.") As we mature and attract a mate, we learn how marvelous the intimate relationship between a man and woman becomes, and how to depend upon and serve each other to the point of becoming "one flesh" as the Bible states it, not only physically, but emotionally and spiritually. That relationship of marriage is the pinnacle of relationship theology. This is why Jesus is called the "Bridegroom," and the "Church" (don't get ahead of me, just keep reading!), which is the entire congregation or number of believers, is called the "Bride of Christ."

Now, we all know that not all of our relationships always work out this nicely. I would venture to say that those relationships not working out is not because God had anything to do with them, but more than likely because we kept Him out and did what we wanted to do. In other words, the reason the relationship failed is one or both parties put self interest ahead of the other. Self. God had nothing to do with the failure of those relationships. Can a broken relationship be restored? Sure! It happens all the time, but not until those interested persons are willing to put someone else ahead of themselves. This humility of spirit, seeking and offering forgiveness and restoration, is absolutely necessary for a reconciled relationship.

God created Man for the express purpose of mutual relationship with him, but gave Man the power of choice and free will. Man chose to break that relationship and has been trying to find his own way by inventing religions and cults of all kinds in an effort to replace that void left by lack of relationship with his Creator.

But relationship with God cannot be found through religion. In fact, religion is the biggest roadblock to seeking a relationship with God. Religion is simply Man trying to reach out to God by doing something that he thinks will please God. "If I can do enough, say enough, pray enough, give enough, sacrifice enough perhaps God will show me favor." <u>Every religion</u> is based upon this "works theology." Neither ceremony, liturgy, creeds, sacraments nor money have ever brought one soul into a reconciled relationship to God. Abstaining from drugs, alcohol, tobacco, illicit sex and the places that provide them is a healthy thing to do but cannot of itself restore a broken relationship with God. Giving up a favorite food or drink, reciting 'program prayers' or self mutilation does nothing to convince or satisfy God.

"But my denomination teaches . . ." Do you really believe that God favors your denomination over others? Quite the contrary; if your denomination professes to be "the only true way," I can pretty well guarantee that it isn't! Do you think that God's intention was to have eleventy-five different denominations of His Church? They can't all be right, and more than likely they're all wrong.

Now, I realize that thus far I have been speaking in terms of Christianity. But the cults such as Islam easily fall precisely under the premise of "God hates Religion;" after all, I observe no one more committed to <u>their religion</u> than an Islamic Fundamentalist. Although the Muslim serves a different god (Allah is not the God of the Bible), he too is seeking to appease his god by *doing.* That is "works-based theology" no matter how you slice it.

So you may be wondering where in the Bible it says that God hates religion. Starting in the Old Testament, I will show you several references and then finish off with what Jesus Christ Himself said concerning religion.

Isaiah 1:13-14 states, *"Bring no more vain oblations; incense is an abomination unto me; the new moons and Sabbaths, the calling of assemblies . . . it is iniquity . . . Your new moons and your appointed feasts my soul hateth: they are a trouble unto me; I am weary to bear them."*

David prays to God in Psalm 40:6, *"Sacrifice and offering thou didst not desire; . . . Burnt offering and sin offering hast thou not required."*

Amos 5:21 says, *"I hate, I despise your feast days, and I will not smell* (the odors of their sacrifices) *in your solemn assemblies."*

Micah 6:6-8 includes, *"Wherewith shall I come before the Lord and bow myself before the high God? Shall I come before him with burnt offerings, with calves of a year old? Will the lord be pleased with thousands of rams, or with ten thousands of rivers of oil? Shall I give my firstborn for my transgression, the fruit of my body for the sin of my soul? He hath showed thee, O man, what is good; and what doth the Lord require of thee, but to do justly, and to love mercy, and to walk humbly with thy God."*[10]

What do you think? Was that on the mark or too strong? I have given you statistics as to how we are doing as a church in reaching or affecting our societies. Are we radically changing our society like the Early Church did? For that matter, are even we as individuals moving from victory to victory, or are we sometimes barely hanging on?

Let me ask you this: does the world need any more cathedrals? Do you remember the Crystal Cathedral in California? Somebody gave over $57 million dollars for the bankrupt "Crystal Cathedral." It was built on the back of big promises and big performances and the sacrificial gifts of those who went there or watched it on television. Does the world need any more "larger than life" evangelists? Some try to convince their audience that "Jets for Jesus" are biblical, with a subliminal message that if they too—follow the formula—they will have similar blessings. How many more sex scandals or financial scams, Catholic or Protestant, will be tolerated or uncovered? Now these things happened on a national scale, but if you are like me you have seen examples of failure and "flesh" on a local level. Please understand me when I say I am not pointing a finger at any of these leaders from a perspective of superiority. It grieves me when things like this take place. I believe the leaders of any of what I mention above never purposely set out to deceive or fail. We are in a battle here in the vineyard of God. It is all too easy to get off track or be misled. Who among us is without sin? Did any of those things make a good and lasting change on our society, or did they perhaps give more *excuses* for many people who need the gospel and real salvation?

Does the world need any more performers or SPECTATORS for that matter? I have been to Jesus festivals in the 1970s as well as many other conferences and concerts in the years following. Some ministries have rented whole football stadiums and spent hundreds of thousands of dollars and pretty much ended up "preaching to the choir." By that I mean, oftentimes, carloads or even busloads of people who are already believers, flock to these things for many different reasons. Some just want to show support for a Gospel work in our secular society. Some want to find renewal or a fresh touch or impartation. I am not saying any one of these things is bad or wrong in itself. I am just asking that we examine these things and listen for the leading of the Lord. Please believe me that when I discover some of the revelations I have come across, it makes me magnify Jehovah at just how merciful he is with us.

I won't tell you other stories of downright deceit I have seen in this country or abroad for that does not lift up anybody. We already know there is an *accuser of the brethren* and I do **not** want to find myself in joint forces with him. But we are also admonished to be wise and wary, and if we hold a position of "watchmen," we must sound an alarm. I will describe to you something I do in some of my leadership sessions. Mind you that most often I am already up on some elevated platform. I told you in the previous chapter how we can thank our friend Constantine for helping add to our already large ego in the style and design of our churches and presentations. See if you can get a mental image of the following:

"Oh my friends, I am so extremely honored to be here with you today. I have traveled many miles and at considerable expense. I want you to know that I have a special message for you. I see you have this lovely Dias for me to address you from." —Note: I am up on a platform with other ministers and sometimes even local politicians. They have no idea what this crazy guy is going to do. If I can, I try to obtain something like a five-gallon pail or, if not, a rickety chair or even speaker box. "My brothers and sisters, I know God has called me. I do hope you understand that even though you have been so welcoming to me, I am still a bit uncomfortable. You see, as I stand on this platform, I am still really at the same level as my colleagues here. Please permit me to stand on this bucket. After all, I am the Reverend Dr. Charles Eddy. Dear friends, I come **humbly** before you today as I stand upon this altar. I would even ask that if any of you, any at all, have a prayer request—please come DOWN to this altar. I said that I have a message and it is this: God told me that this year is unique. It is a special time in your destiny. It is the "Year of the Decimal." That's right. This is 2016 . . . two—zero—one—six. Where are you gonna put the decimal? How bad do you want God's favor in 2016? He told me some of you will sow into this ministry. Obviously, this is good ground—yes? I believe God is saying that if you will give $20.16 a month for 20 months, that he will move that decimal point for you and you will reap your reward of $2016. Glory!! Tell your neighbor, "This is YOUR time."

And I believe that there is somebody out there now who can give a one time love gift of $2016 . . . And **God** is saying, "You just stand back and watch him move that decimal point to the sky!"

Oᴋ—enough is enough. I think I may even feel some nausea forming in the back of my mouth as I recounted this. At this point in my little demonstration, I come back to reality and just speak to the audience no longer "in character." I have watched their faces during this whole ordeal. Some look at me in confusion. Many start smiling, but not quite sure if I'm for real or not, realizing that they have seen some things faintly similar during their journey.

"My friends," I say, "God has not really told me this. But how is it that none of you during the course of my little speech said . . . 'Sir—Did God truly tell you this?—Sir—You said we might come down to an altar. How can any of us come *down* to anything? The floor is level. And Sir—I thought an altar was a place of holiness . . . a place of sacrifice. That looks more like a performance stage. Sir—You look rather stupid standing up there on that bucket.'" I go on to tell them this. "My friends, God <u>has</u> given me a message for you. He is speaking to me and I hope to you. I think he is saying to all of us leaders—Sᴛᴏᴘ! Sᴛᴏᴘ the performance. Stop the show. Stop misrepresenting me. Come down from your platforms and places of honor, and walk among the people as I have walked among you. Humble yourselves so I can use you."

Earlier I told you that in this section of our time together I hoped to come to you as a friend. Friends speak the truth to one another, hopefully in love.

"I no longer call you servants, because a servant does not know his master's business. Instead I have called you

friends, for everything I have learned from my Father I have made known to you."

—John 15:15

I am speaking to you now who are reading this. No longer am I relating an event from a seminar somewhere but am conversing with you. You too must be a leader or called into the Gospel work. Otherwise you would have left me long ago and quit reading this far. I am always more gratified when my book is read than when it is used for a drink coaster or door stop.

The world does not need more performers. Performers too often burn out or die. The world does not need more spectators. Spectators never come into their own unique calling or potential.

James 1:27 tells us, *"Religion that God our Father accepts as pure and faultless is this: to look after orphans and widows in distress, and to keep oneself from being **polluted by the world**."* (Emphasis mine)

Is God speaking to you at all as you read through this material? What do you think Yahweh means by being polluted by the world? Do you think he cares at all if I got something under my fingernails or if I am even tempted to use a foul word on occasion?

Let me bring this chapter toward a close, and I will preface it with Scripture taken from Hebrews.

*"See to it that you do not refuse him who speaks. If they did not escape when they refused him who warned them on earth, how much less will we, if we turn away from him who warns us from heaven? **At that** time his voice shook the earth, but NOW he has promised, 'Once more I will shake not only the earth but also the heavens.' The words 'once more' indicate the **removing** of what can be*

shaken—that is, **created things***—so that what cannot be shaken may remain."*

(Emphasis mine)   —Hebrews 12:25-28

How many of you read the news or watch it on television? Let me ask you a question. Do you think we could quite possibly be in what many call "the last days?" I won't mock you if you do not answer yes. People have been declaring that for longer than I can remember. I, myself, firmly believed I would not be around as long as I have and was convinced I would have been "raptured" by now. But while I do think many have gotten their eschatology wrong, I still believe we are in the culmination of times. Let me describe to you two things that I suggest speak to us of **created things.**

a. Political systems: You read or watch the news. Would you agree that it seems as though governments and political "systems" are being shaken like never before? Where did political systems arise from in Biblical revelation? Did God order that we form governments, or did we demand that we be like other nations or kingdoms? I invite you to search deeper into that study. And yet we watch as nation rises against nation—coupled with the rebellion or turmoil within themselves. Nations worldwide are being shaken!

b. Religious systems: May I suggest to you that **religion** is not Jehovah's invention. As I stated, he initiated relationship. Are the vast varieties of religions, sects, and denominations of the world part of a religious system? Where did that arise from in Biblical revelation? We will develop this more in the next chapter. There is a tremendous "religious" shaking going on!

If indeed we are no longer servants only of Yeshua, and now have come into friendship with him, he declares <u>we should be aware of the Father's business</u>. Let us make every effort then, while we can, to be about the Father's business. I hope I am keeping your attention and interest—*Friend.* ☺

🦅 🦅 🦅

Brain teaser: We are moving along in our skill level and I assure you that this brain teaser is not a trick question. It is not some stupid thing where you might not have listened quite closely enough or I tricked you. It is actually a real problem with a real solution. Yay! You are moving away from little league and toward varsity.

I have to go to market to sell my products. I live in a rather rural area you see, and I am a bit of a gentleman farmer. I have three items that I can manage to carry or herd, but there still remains a problem. I have a fox, a rabbit, and a head of lettuce. The market is just across a lazy but deep river and I must hire a ferry to get myself to market. Here's the rub—The ferry operator is like a mean ogre. He will allow me to only carry one item at a time across the river. Man, he's a greedy jerk! So my problem is this: how do I get my entire product to market—each one in good condition to fetch the best price?

Answer in back.

Chapter 5

Original Intent

I closed the last chapter with the admonition that you and I need to find out what the Father's business is and what we should be doing about it. But some still might think that religion **is** the Father's business . . . and that clergy are really the ones called for such a thing. We know or assume that clergy have usually embarked on some degree of study for such a position. We hope or assume that each take their esteemed position seriously. Yet, even with the best intentions, things can get "complicated." With all the tension between religions in the world and news these days, I hope you will be refreshed by the following story of good will and cooperation.

The Imam and the Confession Booth:

A priest was called away for an emergency. Not wanting to leave the confessional unattended, he called his Muslim Imam friend from across the street and asked him to cover for him. The Imam told him he wouldn't know what to say, but the priest told him to come on over and he'd stay with him for a little bit and show him what to do.

The Imam comes, and he and the priest are in the confessional. After a few minutes a woman comes in and says, "Father—forgive me for I have sinned." Priest: "What did you do?" Woman: "I committed adultery." Priest: "How many times?" Woman: "Three times." Priest: "Say two Hail Mary's—put fifteen dollars in the box and go and sin no more."

A few minutes later a man enters the confessional. He says, "Father forgive me for I have sinned." Priest: "What did you do?" Man: "I committed adultery." Priest: "How many times?" Man: "Three times." Priest: "Say two Hail Mary's—put fifteen dollars in the box and go and sin no more."

The Imam tells the priest that he thinks he's got it, so the priest leaves.

A few minutes later another woman enters and says, "Father forgive me for I have sinned." Imam: "What did you do?" Woman: "I committed adultery." Imam: "How many times?" Woman: "Once."

Imam: **"Go do it two more times. We have a special this week, three for $15."**

I just had to break the tension from that last chapter a little. I hope you enjoyed the humor. I would like to get back on course here though and begin by asking you, "Who is God?" I think almost everybody has an opinion. In my first book, as I introduced apologetics, I state that everybody has a *worldview*. It doesn't matter if you're a college "egghead" or a street corner "crack head;" you have an opinion about what makes the world work the way it does. So who or what is God? Is he Jehovah—the God of the Jewish race and religion? Is he the same god as Allah—the God of the Muslim faith? I am not going to spend time in this book on apologetics. I encourage you to read *The Power of I Will*, or study world religions. You really should be up to speed on such things. I will say only that I do not believe the same as former President George W. Bush. He stated once that we all should get along, especially due to the fact that we serve the same God. I believe that Islam is a Judeo-Christian cult. I believe it is a great counterfeit. But before you give me a "hoorah," let me be the first to say I do not believe the only good Muslim is a dead Muslim. I see so many similarities in our faiths. You may be so appalled by what you hear or see in the news that the thought of us being similar repulses you.

Both Judaism and Islam have a creed or saying, so to speak, that is extremely important and reverent to those who are sincere. The Muslims love to say what is called the Shahada. In Islam, the first of the five pillars is the Shahada. Shahada is the Muslim profession of faith, expressing the two simple, fundamental beliefs that make one a Muslim. "There is no god but Allah and Muhammad is his prophet." Sincere recitation of this confession of faith before two Muslims is the sole requirement for those who wish to join the Muslim community. It represents acceptance not only of Allah and his prophet, but of the entirety of Islam. As one of the Pillars, the Shahada must be recited correctly aloud with full understanding and internal assent at least once in every Muslim's lifetime. The Shahada is also recited in the muzzein's call to prayer, included in the salat (daily ritual prayer) and incorporated in Sufi contemplative prayer. It is also recited in the moments before death. From the Shahada are derived the other fundamental doctrines of Islam: angels, the Quran and the Bible, the prophets, and the Day of Judgment.

The Jewish faith has a creed that is just as sacred as the Shahada. It is said with reverence daily by observant Jews as well as many Messianic Christians who have learned to embrace its beauty. I do not however, ever recall an incident where someone was tortured or beheaded for failure to confess it! It is called the Sh'ma or Shema. The Shema is one of only two prayers that are specifically commanded in the Torah. It is the oldest fixed daily prayer in Judaism, recited morning and night since ancient times. It consists of three biblical passages, two of which specifically say to speak of these things "when you lie down and when you rise up."

Sh'ma Yis'ra'el . . . Adonai Eloheinu . . . Adonai Echad

Hear O Israel, The Lord is our God. The Lord is one.

Both religions claim the Patriarch Abraham as a father in their faith. Muslims may not admit it, but they say they believe in the Torah, Pentateuch, Psalms and Prophets, and the four Gospels. They believe Yeshua was a prophet and even referred to Jews and early Christians as "People of the Book." So how can there be such division? And I have only mentioned two main religions. What about the many other religions of the world? And if that is not confusing enough, many of them have offshoots or sects within themselves. Do you think this is all God's intention? Sometimes Christians can be so smug and almost arrogant. It is like we see the terrible conflicts going on in the world and differing religions and think, "How can they all be so ignorant?" After all, *White is*

Right—right?? And West is best? I say some of these things with a measure of sarcasm. It is not a bad thing to travel outside of one's own country. It helps one get a little perspective of how we differ from other cultures and get a sense of how they view us. We can see Muslims killing other Muslims and think "Sunni—Schmunni" . . . or "What the heck is a Shi'ite?" Let me ask you a question. Do you know the difference between Shi'ite and Sunni? Let me explain it this way, even though I'm sure it is not exhaustive. Sectarian lines can be so complicated. They mix some theology with some politics; add in long standing grudges as well as personal agendas and vendettas. Now throw that together with class struggles and you have the stuff wars have long been made of.

Let us say all the Sunni Muslims in the world had their leader die. If they want to install his successor, they are going to try to find one who is learned in the Koran, the Hadith, and the Sunna. These are their most sacred writings. This, besides other perhaps political characteristics, would make a good candidate. Now let us say the same search is desperately made for a leader of the Shiites. The biggest difference is that this great leader must be proven to be a direct descendant of Muhammad himself. Shia—ti-Ali . . . . "Party of Ali." **Ali** was Muhammad's first cousin and closest living male relative and also married Muhammad's daughter. Shia Muslims believe that Ali was the legitimate successor and eligible as the first caliph since he was the cousin and son-in-law of the Prophet. Have you heard any rumblings about a new global caliphate?

We Christians think something like, "Seriously?—You're all Muslims. Get over yourselves and be civilized like us. We would never act so divisive or foolish." Let me give you another scenario. Suppose the Protestant community all over the world decided it needed one great leader, one unified voice to represent their glorious religion. What kind of candidate would that be? I should think he or she should be well versed in Scripture, holding forth to the basic tenets of the Bible. Perhaps a sound academic profile and resume would be valuable, as well as personal skills. Now, what if the Catholic believers all over the world desire a new grand leader for their religion? Many of the same criterion would apply, except let us not forget that it would be really cool if he was thought to be a direct descendent of Peter. After all, didn't Christ Himself set the standard? *"Thou art Peter. And upon this rock I will build my church"* (Matthew 16:18). You might say I'm splitting hairs. Would you say, "We would at least never fight wars over something as absurd as sectarian or denominational lines?" Think Spanish Inquisition, burning at the stake, and pogroms of all nature. Tens, if not hundreds, of millions of souls have been slaughtered in the name of the Christian God. Please take a look at what was known as the Thirty Year War between Protestants and Catholics. I know of people even now, who try to do evangelistic work in Ireland and that area of Europe who state there is great difficulty in breaking down the hatred and animosity that still exists between the faiths. We need not feel Islam has anything on us. Is all of this mess God's *original intent?*

🦆 🦆 🦆

This has been a bit heavy so let me ask you a simple question. Was God competent? I mean have you ever thought of that before? Here he is . . . *Ex Nihilo* . . . Out of nothing, he creates this whole world. Everything we interface with. Everything we think, see, or smell he created. Boom! I'd say he is pretty competent!

Let me ask you this next. So he was competent, but was he lonely? Did you ever think of that? This God . . . since before there was time . . . He's there . . . Is he lonely? I don't think so—but yet I don't think he was quite complete. Not in a whiny or lacking way—more of a "there's something more" to this grand plan, kind of way. This will make a little more sense as we go on in understanding *Original Intent*. When thinking "origin," it only makes sense to go back to the beginning.

Genesis ~ noun, plural **gen-e-ses**
    1. an origin, creation, or beginning

Let's see if the Holy Scripture sheds any light on God's original intent starting back in the book of Genesis. Genesis 1:26 reads, *"Then God said, Let us make man in* OUR *image . . . ."* (Emphasis mine). I told you that I love learning about the Hebrew roots of our faith. The word "God" there in Hebrew is **Elohiym**. It is a plural noun. Right off the bat Yahweh is giving us an important lesson. This builds a good case for the doctrine or concept of the Trinity. How can one entity alone say, "Let US make man in OUR image?" Jehovah himself dwells in *community* or "family," so to speak. Each part of the Godhead is in perfect relationship and builds up the other. I can just hear the Father bragging on the Son, "Behold my Son with whom I am well pleased." And the Son saying, "Call no man good—only the Father is good." And all the time, Ruach ha Kodesh (Holy Spirit) is causing praise to rise up in the hearts of ALL creation.

So Elohiym created man—he had **relationship** with him. What a wonderful garden paradise it had to have been. Imagine the beauty. Imagine the perfect harmony there would have been; because, at that time, sin had not entered into the picture and begun its destructive consequences. Yet the plan in the heart of Jehovah was not complete. He created man.

Who is Adam? Do you believe there even was such a person? Muslims believe there was and so do Jews as well as many Christians. Do you think we all evolved out of primordial ooze, or was there actually a real person whom genealogy can be traced back to?

Was Adam competent? I asked you this question regarding Yahweh and the answer should be pretty much . . . Duh! eeYah! Well let me refresh your knowledge a little regarding Adam. The bible gives us clues as to how big the original **Garden** of Eden was. We are given the names and geographical areas, as well as its description as stretching from the Tigris to the Euphrates Rivers. It was no small piece of real estate. Imagine managing this huge paradise garden. I mean really, imagine that YOU were the sole caretaker of the state or province you live in right now. Our Creator, so wonderful and yet so empowering. If I had created that garden I might have micro-managed just a little. Besides making sure you appreciated all I had done, when introducing the King of Beasts I may have said, "See that amazing creature? I created that. You shall call its name Lion. And that flying creature that effortlessly does what you may only dream of . . . you shall call Eagle."

> *"Now the Lord God had formed out of the ground all the beasts of the field and all the birds of the air. He brought them to the man **to see what he would name them;** and whatever the man called each living creature, that was its name."*
>
> (Emphasis mine)   —Genesis 2:19

Imagine the mental prowess of Adam to have named all those creatures, to know each by name as well as its place and function in the garden. I would definitely say Adam was competent. Adam was **lord** over his domain.

I asked you before if God was lonely. Now I ask you if Adam was lonely. Yahweh recognized Adam's need before he did. How could Adam yearn for some creature he had never before seen or known? He doesn't know a soft curvaceous looking "hottie" from a can of paint. Neither had been invented yet! Just as Jehovah (Elohiym) was in relationship, he wanted Adam to be **complete**. Yahweh stated, like a loving Father, "It is not good for man to be alone." To this day he knows our need before we do.

Here's a stupid question. Did Adam ever sleep? Did Adam have a place to lay his head? I imagine Adam and God had a certain period of time when it was just them hanging out in the Garden. I think it probably took more than one shift for Adam to view, inspect, and name all of the beasts of the field and the birds of the air. So I propose to you that our friend Adam had more than a night or two under the stars to sleep. Did Adam have a place to lay his head? Before you decide to make a drink coaster of this book, let me assure you I am going somewhere with this line of questioning.

> . . ."But for Adam no suitable helper was found. So the Lord God caused the man to fall into a deep sleep, and while he was sleeping, he took one of the man's ribs and closed up the place with flesh."
> —Genesis 2:20-21

Again I encourage you to stop once in a while and not just plow on to the next verse in your devotion time. I looked up the Hebrew meaning for that term "deep sleep." It does not mean that Adam was really whooped and he fell into some nice REM-pattern sleep. It implies the Lord caused him to go into a deep, supernatural sleep.

Jehovah pierced his side, right? He took out a rib and closed up the place with flesh. Adam was now complete . . . almost!

Note: out of man—he took the **material** needed to make a mate. This is what Adam needed to be **complete.** God's original intent seems to have been this: The Godhead—in perfect relationship with His creation (Adam and Eve)—created offspring to fill the earth with **family**—forever.

The Jewish Shema is beautiful and I recite it often. "Adonai Eloheinu" (possessive plural of Elohiym)—this tripartite Unit—is "Adonai Echad"—is ONE! Knowing some of this beautiful language of the bible helps one to appreciate Scripture more.

> *"For this reason a _man_ will leave his _father_ and **mother***
> (a unit of three parts) *and be united with his wife, and*
> *they will become one flesh."*
> (Emphasis mine)—Genesis 2:24

That same word Moses uses in Genesis for the term one flesh is that Hebrew word "Echad." It speaks of unity. For those who preach and like to develop such things, one could also teach a little from this on the sacred union of man and woman. It is not just "hooking up" or something casual and inconsequential. Something mystical and powerful happens at sexual union. It is as God designed it. Another part of His original intent.

The Beginning of Religion

Genesis 2:25 tells us, *"The man and his wife were both naked, and they felt no shame."*

A band called Enigma popularized a song titled, "Return to Innocence." I like the musical arrangement as well as the Indian chanting in it, as it makes me feel peaceful and alludes to a state of innocence, in my mind. As I stated, I love the concept of returning to a place of innocence, purity and tenderness. I find that the older one grows in life, the harder it is to not become a bit cynical or skeptical. I do, however, take a small exception with some of the words in the song. It sounds like we have all the answers within us, when they sing for us to—"return to yourself." Perhaps I am just not working the formula correctly? Many modern day preachers would have us believe that if we only worked the Christian "formula" properly, we would somehow lead prosperous and relatively pain free lives. Sorry—off chasing a squirrel again.

Studies have shown that when a marriage is healthy, it is often like that original account in Genesis. It is ideal when a husband and wife can find themselves naked, in <u>every</u> sense, and yet feel no shame. But if sin creeps in . . . if there is deception . . . if there is betrayal . . . oftentimes, a covering up or hiding becomes evident. Lights need to be turned off. Take your own turn in the bathroom. You have your secrets and I have mine. Innocence is lost.

In Genesis 3:10-11, Adam says to God when called, *"I heard you in the garden, and I was afraid, because I was naked; so I hid."* Jehovah answers . . . *"Who told you that you were naked?"*

Sin had now entered the picture . . . innocence was lost . . . relationship was broken. We see an example of how religion was born. All religion is some sort of system of works—some system of appeasing or earning our place before God. Note how man tried on his own to cover up his nakedness.

Genesis 3:7 says, "*They sewed fig leaves together and made coverings for themselves.*" Later in the chapter we read, "*The Lord God made garments of skin for Adam and his wife and clothed them.*"
—Genesis 3:21

As is my habit, I pondered this a bit. I also looked up a couple words in Hebrew. So I sez to myself I sez, "Humm—Garments of skin?—Something seems to have had to die? Blood must have been shed?" and, "I wonder what that word garment is in the original language?" Come to find out, garments there mean a "cloak or tunic." This is not just some shabby cloth to cover their private parts. Do you see how even in the beginning Yahweh is teaching us? The bible says that without the shedding of blood there can be no remission or forgiveness of sin. It also states that when he forgives us he clothes us in robes of righteousness! This feeble attempt also shows that even when we sin, God is merciful and provides a covering. Man's way is partial and with guilt. Fellowship is lost or strained at best. Even in the beginning God is not asking more from us than he has already **more** than demonstrated. He is merciful. He is longsuffering. He is all of the things he declares himself to be in 1 Corinthians chapter 13. That is the "Love" chapter. You should sometime try and substitute the word "love" there and insert Yeshua or God. It refers to Agape love. That is the God kind of love that is his nature as well as what he imparts to us when we receive him as Lord.

Much more could be said on the topic of religion. I made mention in previous chapters, as well as gave scripture references, in regard to religion and the traditions of man. Suffice it to say that it was not Yahweh's original intent. He was not the author of religion, and **it** never has . . . nor ever will save men from the power or curse of the fall.

So we have us a real problem. God's original intent was to have a relationship with man. Man sinned and messed up the whole thing. Did God wring his hands in frustration or give up? Man kind of knew he messed up. Man kind of, in his heart, knew God still desired a relationship with us. And we, who are so good at thinking up ways of our own to please Him, came up with a perfect solution. Let's put God in a box—or at least a building. I want you to note an interesting wording in 2 Chronicles 6. Solomon is dedicating the Temple after it is finished. In verse 41 he says this: *"Now arise O Lord God, and come to your resting place."* I wonder if God was tired. Why did he need a place to rest? Did God need to sleep? Just hang on to that thought. ☺

A Move toward Relationship

Who was this man Jesus? Is it ok for me to call him Yeshua? Do you believe there really was an actual person in time and history other than the occasional professional baseball player from the Dominican Republic? I'm kidding of course. Muslims believe there was a real historical figure called Jesus. They call him Isa . . . Isa Ibn Maryam . . . to be more specific; Jesus, son of Mary. I'd like then, to ask you several of the same questions about Yeshua as I posed regarding God or Adam.

Do you think Yeshua was anything like Adam or a "type" of Adam? Have you ever thought of him in that regard? Do you think he was lord of his domain? I more than *kind of* think he was. He raised the dead. He walked on water. He healed the lame, blind and deaf. Yes Sir, I think he was both competent and Lord of his domain. He had power over nature. Even storms obeyed his commands to be at peace!

Dumb questions still are being asked. Did Yeshua ever sleep? We reckoned that Adam must have slept, but how about Jesus?

He started his public ministry around age thirty, it is said. This ministry and the recorded public miracles took place during about a three year period, right? Do you think he laid down at night and often had a good rest?

Was the Messiah lonely? Not in a whiny sort of way, but rather in a not quite complete sort of way. As if something still were lacking in His perfect plan and purpose.

Read Matthew 8:18-20 (vs. 20), *"Foxes have holes and birds of the air have nests, but the Son of Man has no place to lay his head."* As I have said before, we need to think on things as we race through scripture. What an odd thing to say to the teacher of the law. Could it mean a lot more than an admonition to toughen up? Was Yeshua telling them to be prepared to rough it and sleep on the ground?

The Son of Man was competent. He was certainly lord of his domain. He ruled over men and nature. But he was still not complete—or at least his mission was not complete.

1 Corinthians 15:45 gives us another title or role He fulfilled. So it is written, *"The first man Adam became a living being, the last Adam, a life giving spirit. The spiritual did not come first, but the natural, and after that the spiritual. The first man was of the dust of the earth, the second man from heaven. As was the earthly man, so are those who are of the earth, and as is the man from heaven, so also are those who are of heaven."*

Yahweh's original intent was to have eternal fellowship and relationship with his creation. Christ Jesus—Yeshua—the last or 2nd Adam, came to carry out to everlasting completion the Father's will. Again the Father knew . . . it is not good for the "second Adam" . . . the Son of Man . . . to dwell alone.

Did Christ die when they laid him in the tomb? Of course I want to emphasize that **he physically died on that cross.** But we are told that during that time he "led captivity captive" and "descended into the lower parts of the earth." I am not going to go into that debate more here, but I believe it supports an opinion. Do you really think anything could annihilate the Spirit of Yeshua? I believe that at the moment of conception a human body becomes an eternal soul. Certainly the Son of God lives forever. But may I suggest that like the first Adam—the second was not eternally dead—but in a deep sleep, so to speak—a deep, supernatural sleep. During the crucifixion, he too had his side pierced. Out of his side gushed blood and water.

I would like to take a short detour into something I think is important. Throughout this book I have encouraged you to consider exploring the Hebrew roots to our Christian faith. Look at things not only as they are written to us in whatever particular translation you have; but look at Scripture through the lens of Jews who are writing to other Jews—and by his grace, to us who are grafted in. I reminded us that the Early Church did not celebrate Yeshua's birth (Christmas). But that in no way means they dismiss the beautiful truth of the virgin birth and Messiah's coming. They would more likely assume that he came around what we call September or October, when they celebrated the Feast of Tabernacles. Indeed John's narrative tells us, *"The Word became flesh and dwelt (tabernacled) among us"* John 1:14. I have given you historical backing to help understand that the Early Church was persecuted because they celebrated Passover. So I want to ask your opinion about a certain scripture. Why does John, writing under the inspiration of the Holy Spirit, word John 19:35 the way he does? **He tells us the truth and he testifies so that we "might believe."** He already told us earlier that the soldiers found that **Jesus was dead.** Roman soldiers would not be in the habit of taking a living man down from the cross mistakenly thinking he was dead! Was John trying to tell his brothers in the faith, "Really guys—I saw it—he was dead?" Tragic as this was, this is not what made John want to shout the good news from the housetops. When you take communion at your church, please remember that this is not what (some say) good Baptists do at the beginning of each month. "This, do in remembrance of me" is more like, "When you come together to celebrate the wonderful Feast of Passover, know that it ALL speaks of me."

The Blood and Water Issue

Ask yourself why it was when the Jews demanded of Yeshua, *"What miraculous sign can you show us to prove your authority to do all this?" Yeshua answered them, "Destroy this temple, and I will raise it again in three days"* (Fulfillment of John 2:19-21). Why didn't he tell them they would witness and hear accounts of the blind seeing and dead being raised? John was Jewish. He grew up in the faith. John was also familiar with the Roman Empire. Yeshua was certainly not the first person to be crucified by the Romans or the last. Hundreds of men were crucified at different times for different reasons. John was not interested in merely informing readers of another crucifixion but, rather, that this particular one was intimately related to the Temple. John is the only New Testament writer that mentions the Kidron Valley. Is that coincidental or had that valley made an impression upon him?

Temple Sacrifices, the Blood Drains, and Water

Sacrifice was nothing new to John. Sacrifices and their consequent outflow of blood and water were essential to the Temple's existence. As a result, thousands of gallons or liters of water had to be used for the animal blood that had to be disposed of. But how? It was accomplished by being poured into a drain at the "base of the altar" (Leviticus 1:11, 13; 4:7, 18, 25, 30, 34), a rule that applied to both tabernacle and temple. For instance, the First Temple (Solomon's) required ten lavers of water for rinsing blood from sacrificial offerings, (II Chronicles 4:6). Therefore, in the Second Temple of John's day, large amounts of water were poured into the altar's drainage system to flush away the blood of lambs. Since the Temple Mount was a hill with a flat limestone surface, where did the drains empty? They spewed into the Kidron Valley below.

Yeshua captured the essence of that Temple on the cross and John finally got it. The glorious truths that he learned as a disciple of the Master begin exploding in his heart and mind. He stayed when others fled. He beheld with his own eyes the death of his beloved friend and Master. They had just finished celebrating Passover. "My word," read (my WORD)—"He told us his body would be broken. He told us he would be a sacrifice for many. He is the Lamb without blemish. He is our Passover. He does cleanse us and take away all our guilt and shame. I must go tell the others . . . so that they too might believe!"

"Unless you be born again . . . not born of a woman . . . but born in the Spirit . . . you can never enter the kingdom of heaven." In Luke 23:46 Yeshua called out in a loud voice, *"Father, into your hands I commit my spirit."* The apostle John says it this way in John 19:30, *"It is finished"* and he gave up his spirit. The Father knew His son was perfect, but the mission was not yet complete. Out of our Lord's own body came the very material to build a suitable mate. Remember the account in Genesis where the Lord said that Abel's blood cried out from the ground? How much more is the cry and the consequence of Messiah's blood?

I suggest to you that out of Messiah's obedience and the "cry" of His blood come the material to build a perfect mate. We know that Jehovah took the material from Adam . . . fashioned it and breathed life into it . . . and created Eve. I suggest that out of those called to become disciples . . . on the day of Pentecost . . . the church—the second Eve, was born. God breathed the Holy Spirit into the Bride he prepared for his Son. We know that we are called the Bride of Christ. We are the second Eve, the mystical bride God created to fulfill his original intent.

He, Yeshua, is the head. We are to be married into Him. We together are to have offspring and fill the whole earth with His glory. Every time we lead some new believer into the Kingdom, we have brought new sons and daughters in Zion into the world. We now have continual relationship to God. We now can embrace our position . . . not as a religion . . . not as a slave or a concubine . . . but as wife and helpmate. We are co-heirs to all the promises and power of the Godhead.

I would like to say just a little more about our being the Bride of Christ. We are admonished that a beautiful bride is one without spots or wrinkles. That speaks of work on our part of inner cleansing. We are to be holy and without blemish.

"Let us rejoice, and give honor to him: the marriage of the Lamb is come, and His wife has made herself ready."
—Revelation 19:7

"We shall all be changed in a moment, in a twinkling of an eye—at the last trumpet."
—1 Corinthians 15:51-52

This is speaking of our physical bodies. Too often Christians have this subliminal concept that, when they get to heaven, they will automatically become perfect in every way. We think it is a call back into legalism and away from grace for someone to suggest that we have a part in our sanctification or that it is needful at all. Knowing this may help you appreciate a deeper message to us that is found in the book of Esther. There once was a great king. He could have had any beautiful maiden in his domain. Do you think that when he spotted the beautiful virgin Esther he said, "Bring her here"—with her instantly, "in the twinkling of an eye," becoming a bride worthy of him? He had plenty of wives, not to mention concubines. Scripture tells us, in this case, the call came with a caveat. When Ester was being prepared as a bride for her king she went through a time of preparation. Scripture tells us she went through a whole year—purifying the flesh. Six months were spent in the application of oils—and six months with "sweet odors" (spices). The oil speaks of the work of the Holy Spirit. The spices speak of the fruit of the Spirit. See Esther 2:12.

We are to be found with our lamps full of Holy Spirit oil. We are to be trimmed and ready, eager to be with our beloved. Do you think John had a hard time grasping this concept? It may seem a bit feminine or foreign for us men to comprehend. I do not think so. Scripture describes him as the one leaning on the Master's breast. He himself boasts in John 21:20, *"the disciple whom Jesus loved."*

Today, does the Son of Man have a place to rest his head? Scripture records him asking that question back in Matthew 8 and He is asking that still of us. Is he tired? Was Solomon making a place where Jehovah can rest? That word "head" in Greek does not mean his melon or anatomical head. I think it means his position . . . His authority . . . His Priesthood. He wants to rest His head as Head of His church . . . the body of Christ. He wants you!

When in these last days and distressing times, you become confused—as the "religious system" is being shaken like never before—when you see all manner of deception and strong delusion—remember Father's original intent. Jehovah's original intent was simplicity, innocence, and relationship. Simple and innocent does not necessarily mean superficial or shallow. His is a call of infinite depth and intimacy. Find yourself simply cultivating your garden . . . your marriage relationship to the Son of Man . . . Yeshua ha Meshiach. Jesus the Messiah!

Brain teaser:

You are doing well on your journey so far young Jedi. Please take a moment to practice your skill with an easy riddle. You will need the force to be strong with you for the one at the end of the next chapter.

Can you name three consecutive days without using the words Wednesday, Friday, or Sunday?

Answers in the back.

Chapter 6

H. E. Double
Hockey Sticks

This next chapter has been simmering within me for a long time. I mentioned that one of the main reasons for me writing this book is because I have grown in my thinking as well as theology. While the following seems a position I must declare, it feels risky. There is a subject that almost nobody preaches on in today's meetings. As a writer, I know that my volume of sales goes down exponentially with certain subject matter. Cookbooks, mystery or romance novels, and the like lead the industry by far in sales and revenue. As far as the Christian book market goes, one can sell plenty of copies of Christian romance or a lovely book about a child who has been to heaven and back. Not one person appears to say, "Don't you be talking about Heaven, and shame on you for even using that word."

Politics and Religion—subjects Momma told me NOT to bring up, have both found a way into my book and life. Have you ever seen the cartoon where an employee is seen with his head in a vise? As it is being turned and he is in anguish, he tells the other character (who appears to be his boss), "Give it another turn you

95

S@&." I hope I don't have a similar demeanor and certainly don't want to carry a death wish; and yet I press on in this chapter.

Even now as I write this,—*"oh no . . . I think it's gonna happen"*—it is as if there are voices in my—*"make him shut up"*—head. There is a strong desire—*"we're gonna pay for this"*—for me to just write a lovely story about that child who went to Heaven. *"Don't tell me I didn't try to stop him."* But no, the subject matter—*He's gonna blow"*—is too important. The Hell with it, I'm "goin in."

What the hell is hell?

If I listen to what I have heard around me I get more than a little confused. It's cold as hell this January. Just you wait—July will be hot as hell.

Those Patriots seem to put a hell of a team together every year, and yet no way in hell will my team make it to the playoffs.

She's cuter than hell. He's tough as hell. Hell yes! Hell no! I could go on. . . .

I could go on I'm sure, but the voices have stopped and I think I made my point. Besides that, some have already now decided this book should've been used as a door stop. "How dare a religious man even use such language?" Oh, one more expression comes to mind. "Sure as hell." Are you really so sure of what you proclaim . . . to be **so sure** of?

Before I go any further I want to make clear to you, the reader, some of my core beliefs. I believe in hell and will do my best to define that to you. Most importantly, I believe there is only ONE plan for salvation. Jesus came in the form of a man and purchased our right standing with God and our eternal hope. All religions do not lead to the same place. Well, actually I kind of believe all *religions* do lead to the same place—frustration, confusion, emptiness, and hopelessness. Only a relationship and new life in the Messiah can assure us of what Jehovah's original intent has always been.

I came across a book a while back that I honestly don't even know how it got in my suitcase. I will be referencing it in this chapter. It's a wonderful work and far more elaborate and detailed than I will bring in here. I was so moved that I read it a second time. I even called the author personally to make sure I was not missing his message and somehow reading something into it. I pray often that I will not be deceived, and we are told in Scripture to test all things. His insights allowed me to dust off my concepts of hell and really begin to wrestle with certain issues. As I said, almost no Christian preachers address this topic, and I do not find other faiths or religions any more eager to wade in with their commentary or opinion. Everybody seems to go about their business with almost an unspoken agreement that we believe alike. Yet NOBODY really lives like it.

"Father God, I have some real questions about hell and about death. Is it going to knock you off your throne if I process them with you?"

Scenario One:

Let's take this one scenario, I need you to follow along and decide if I have it about right. I'm a young college student. I was brought up in a Christian home but was not totally sure if I wanted or needed the faith I was raised up in. But, as God so often does, I was drawn to a good university that happened to be a Christian liberal arts college. It was during my first year, after being required to go to chapel . . . after meeting other young students and faculty who truly loved God . . . that I found myself really digging into the Bible and seeking Him and truth. (So far this was my life.)

One week an amazing Christian band and ministry came to our college campus. They were going to be there for two nights performing and preaching. I invited a friend who was what we call "unsaved" to come along. You should have seen it. It was awesome. The group performed many of their favorites that have become popular in our worship services. But what moved me the most was their explanation of scripture and even how people our age think. They said things about God and living for Jesus that sounded so compelling, and I hoped my friend was listening. They said God loves us. It does not matter what we have done or been through, God will accept us as we are. They told us that Christ died a horrible death on a cross so that, by believing in Him, we could live forever in heaven. NOTHING could separate us from the love of God. Man, it was powerful. They gave an invitation call at the end for anybody who wanted more information, or those who wanted to make Jesus their Lord and Savior, to come forward. I was discouraged when my buddy did not respond. I asked him about it when we left the auditorium. He told me that he almost did go forward. He said he wanted to go back the next night and hear them again just to make sure they aren't "forcing people or making this junk up." He lived off campus so I said I'd catch him tomorrow and went to my dorm.

The next day on campus and during that night I looked all over for my friend. I found out the shocking news that on his way home the night before, he was in a terrible car wreck and did not survive.

You may get where I'm going with this. Did I misrepresent a typical gathering and a typical Christian altar call? Is it not true that our loving heavenly Father would indeed, have welcomed my friend into the Kingdom that night? How is it that this loving God would seemingly change his character so drastically on my friend? Now, less than twenty four hours later, will that same God allow—some would say send—my friend to go to everlasting torment?

Scenario Two:

One of my undergraduate majors was Psychology. The other major was Sociology. Suffice it to say, I like learning how the mind works and I love watching people. I have had the privilege of working with the mentally impaired and handicapped as part of my studies as well as life experience. I have some questions and I'd like some answers. All of us believe God is merciful, and we know scripture tells us his loving kindness lasts forever. We have a real hard time thinking Jehovah would allow or send someone to hell that is innocent. The kind of person I mean here is somebody who has not yet done anything wrong or sinful. Would anybody believe that the miscarried baby goes to hell? How about the sweet little three year old? What about someone who has not yet reached the age of accountability? And just what is that age?

God will certainly not send a mentally handicapped person to hell. I wonder then, just what is the level of cognition, before judgment is pronounced and sentence delivered? I wonder if a sinner with an IQ of 122 will be held to a different scale from the poor guy who is mild-mentally retarded . . . or say about an IQ of 50–55. What about the girl who was real sharp and had a traumatic brain injury before making her first communion? These are hard enough decisions to make regarding placement in school, which lasts a few years . . . let alone an endless eternity! Life is difficult here in our society with some of the above conditions. But if it assures me that I will not burn forever and forever, sign me up. Why in the world would I want to risk losing my salvation by living a relatively normal life? Maybe when every eye was closed and every head bowed, I didn't get my hand up high enough to appease such a God. Maybe I had me a good salvation going, and then that lustful thought I had became a direct ticket to the fires of hell! Did not our Lord say in Mark 9:47, "*If your eye causes you to sin, pluck it out. It is better to enter the Kingdom of God with one eye than to have two eyes and be thrown into hell . . . ?*" God, is this really what that passage is trying to convey? And if it is, why does nobody really live as though it is true?

Scenario Three:
I love being involved with the amazing nation of India. Studies tell us that it will not be long before they will be the most populous people group on the planet with over a billion souls. I and many others are doing our best—well not truly our best if we believe the mainline doctrine of hell—to bring the gospel to them. There is just no way in the world we are going to reach all those souls in time, even with the advancement of the internet and cell phones. We will just not be able to deliver a

good presentation of the message of salvation to all those masses of humanity. Plus, since you have commanded we go into the entire world, some of the responsibility of their eternal future falls on me. How can I bring them the gospel where they can make a cognitive and whole-hearted decision to make you their Lord and Savior? Somebody told me that God never **sends** anyone to hell . . . the person **chooses** to go to hell and spend eternity there as a consequence of his or her own free will. God, is that true or was that person full of bologna?

🕊 🕊 🕊

In the next few pages I will try to present from scripture many good reasons and proofs that we must reexamine some of the long held beliefs about hell. I urge you to keep one thing in mind almost as though they were lenses that force you to see something a certain way. Look at all of the following through the lens that **God is love**. Not only the premise that God is love, but that **God is just**.

Sometimes we can read the bible and yet we have our own preconceived view of the "voice" behind what is said. Let me give you and example.

> "Do not be deceived; God cannot be mocked. A man reaps what he sows."
> —Galatians 6:7

One can read the above passage with a "mess up and you'll be squashed like a bug" voice behind it. Or at least something like, "Nana nana boo boo—You're getting what is coming to you." And do not be mistaken, the scripture that follows speaks of reaping eternal life. What if we could read and accept that verse as simply a matter of fact?

In a different example, let us say that I decide to get up on the roof of my house. I am too cheap to hire a younger man to fix that shingle that is coming loose, so I am determined to do it myself. After all God has given me years of experience and I still have the ladder and means to do it. Besides that, I have scripture to guide me. "God helps those who help themselves." (You won't find that scripture in case you've heard it before.) As bad luck would have it, I get dizzy and fall off the edge of my roof and break my noggin. Would anybody feel a big angry god caused that misfortune? If I recount it later in life, would someone say it is only because I had a warped view of God? Instead, they might rephrase the laws of nature to me this way: "Do not be deceived; gravity cannot be mocked. A cheapskate reaps what he sows." Is gravity angry or punitive? Of course not. It is just a rule of nature . . . an absolute. It is just part of God's will as it relates to creation. He spoke it all into existence by the power of his will, and it all has a perfect function in his plan. No one would object if I state absolutely, "Only a fool declares in his heart there is no gravity." Yet the world thinks the Scripture is in error when it states, "A fool says in his heart, there is no God." I encourage you to consider that God is love. He is sovereign and He is a just God.

🦆 🦆 🦆

"Love never fails" (1 Corinthians 13:8)! Words of victory, power, hope and encouragement. Oh, do we dare believe? Can it really be possible? For most of my life, I have embraced teachings built on well-defined arguments for why LOVE SOMETIMES FAILS. Not that it wanted to fail or lacked the power to succeed; it just didn't work out sometimes. In fact, it didn't work out most of the time."

—David Nuckols

Not too long ago I was invited to work alongside a different ministry in a country I am very fond of. I tried my best to fill the role they had for me. During that time I made acquaintances with the leadership and, in the course of conversation, made known a couple of my beliefs. I made sure not to reveal anything I thought could be controversial or divisive with the people they served. After all, we agree on far more than the few things we disagree with. I felt a bit of a cold shoulder while there but was not expecting what I got later. I was told by email that they will not invite me back ever again, and they prefer I not mention to anyone my affiliation with their group or their ministry. In fact, they assure me they will pray for me that I see and **repent** from the error in my doctrine. Didn't see that coming! I must admit I like being liked. It hurts me to be rejected and I take it quite seriously. I usually spend quite a bit of time in prayer asking Father to reveal to me where I am wrong. Admonitions like, "Wounds from a friend are better than kisses from an enemy" . . . and "consider others as better than yourself" . . . are verses that come to mind. Knowing my Savior was despised and rejected also comes to mind. Though I don't want to bring it on myself for being a jerk, I wonder if they believe that if I do not repent I will be cast into the Lake of Fire. I don't mean to sound like I harbor offense. But if you truly believed that, would you not make a serious effort to rescue the one perishing? The bible does say that narrow is the way that leads to eternal life, and **few** there are who will find it.

"When a leading evangelical like Dr. A. W. Tozer thinks that 90% of the **members of our churches** are lost, we are in trouble!

Even Billy Graham was quoted as saying that 85% of our **church members** are lost! These are frightening figures. If they come anywhere near being correct, **you** may be in trouble."[12] That's out of the flock that proclaim themselves born again. If we even dismiss it as being too restrictive and raise their numbers to say, 40% being saved . . . we have to allow that 60% will burn forever. And this does not account for the billions lost from other faiths, nor multitudes gone before throughout the ages!

I wrote the book *The Power of I Will* and I think it is a fine and a useful tool in reaching people. But, in retrospect, I believe now that I diminished the awesomeness of God's will and elevated that of man. How Greek thinking of me. "Adonia Echad" . . . The Lord is One. The Trinity is not God, the Devil, and the will of man. That is polytheism. There is Jehovah and none other.

- Is the power of our "free will" to damn ourselves for eternity really absolute, exceeding the power of God's "free will" to save us, his very own property? "All souls are mine" (Ezek. 18:4). If so, who suffers most in eternal damnation: man or God who loves man with an everlasting love (Jer. 31:3)?

- How can Christ be considered greater than Adam if Adam has the power to condemn more people than Christ has the power to save?

Black Lives Matter! Police Lives Matter! These are slogans that are currently in the news, and many are trying to broaden the narrative by saying All Lives Matter. I am suggesting to you that All Souls Matter. This has been called blasphemy by some but the "Blessed Hope" by those of us who have researched it and now embrace it. Blessed and glorious hope. I urge you to study it for yourself. Please pray about your conclusion and accept nothing that cannot clearly be backed by scripture. What is right or just about a punishment that never ends? How has this teaching affected the spreading of the "Good News"—the Gospel? Think about it. An "eternal" hell . . .

- maligns God's character before the world.
- contradicts His unending and unfailing love for all people.
- makes our worship stem more from fear than of true affection.
- denies His unlimited power to accomplish all His will.
- infinitely minimizes Christ's triumph over death and the evil one.
- denies that Christ fully accomplished His mission on earth.
- negates the most glorious promises in the Bible.
- ignores the testimony of the early church. *(see Notes: in bibliography)

We spent a whole chapter on some of the history of the Early Church. Early Messianic believers predominately believed that any "hell" Yeshua spoke about would have been a time or place of purification and not an endless place of torture. Their Jewish tradition and belief would hold the same conclusions. The Old Covenant is full of examples regarding the mercy and **justice** of Jehovah.

In *Abraham Lincoln the Christian*, William Johnson, stated:

Abraham Lincoln did not nor could not believe in the endless punishment of anyone of the human race. He understood punishment for sin to be a Bible doctrine; that the punishment was parental in its object, aim, and design, and intended for the good of the offender;

hence it must cease when justice is satisfied. All that was lost by the transgression of Adam was made good by the atonement.[13]

We have already dealt with **traditions of men** earlier in our conversations. May I again remind you of the Holy Scriptures, (Matt. 15:6,9), where our Master chastises people regarding sacred tradition.

"Thus you nullify the word of God for the sake of your tradition . . ." and *"They worship me in vain, their teachings are but rules taught by men."*

Let me give you an example of what holding fast to tradition, and even our own experience, does to our theology. We know in our hearts that endless punishment and torture just doesn't sound like anything we would want to assign as coming from our god. Yes, I used a little "g" for God and we have loads of them. Perhaps we even know a gay person or two, or we watch a favorite television program with that lifestyle in it.

"Do you not know that the wicked will not inherit the kingdom of God? Do not be deceived; neither the sexually immoral nor idolaters nor adulterers nor male prostitutes nor homosexual offenders nor thieves nor the greedy nor drunkards nor slanderers nor swindlers will inherit the kingdom of God. And that is what some of you were."
—1 Cor. 6:9-11

Maybe I have already offended your theology and personal opinion. Furthermore, you may feel I am singling out homosexuals. Let me see if it is hard to find something that hits a little closer to home in our own lives.

"For of this you can be sure: No immoral, impure or greedy person—such a person is an idolater—has any inheritance in the kingdom of Christ and of God."
—Eph. 5:5

Do you still not find yourself in the list above? Remember the scripture I quoted about those who have had a lustful thought? Rats!—Now we are all having a hard time reading the rest of my book after "plucking out an eye" so as not to enter Hades with both.

Do you understand what I said then about nullifying the Word of God? Because we pay lip service to a tradition of hell that may not be accurate, we charge God with all manner of mischief. We declare that indeed those who dabble in any or even all of the sins mentioned above will still somehow deserve heaven. We may not say it, but we essentially put ourselves in the position of judge. We declare that heaven will be filled with people who were essentially, good "ole" boys and girls.

Remember my admonition to turn off that "angry God" filter when we read scripture. Remember I told you, "Do not be deceived—gravity will not be mocked." If we would only embrace this Blessed Hope, it would be so much easier to worship God and take him at his word. The Kingdom of God—on earth as it is in heaven—will have no sin, stain, spot or wrinkle in it. Kingdom life on earth calls for it and Yahweh has made provision for all of heaven to be filled only with his glory. He has made a way for us. No other faith or religion of the world holds this **hope** or this **promise**. If we can wrap our brains around the love of God, maybe we can also see his love—in his justice.

I have called us to "return to innocence" in response to what I read in the Bible. In Matthew 18:3 Jesus says, *"I tell you the truth, unless you change and become like little children, you will never enter the kingdom of heaven. Therefore, whoever humbles himself like this child is the greatest in the kingdom of heaven.*" Still, later on in that chapter is the part about plucking out your eye to avoid the fires of hell. All of this speaks of heaven and the kingdom of God. A basic axiom of bible school training and good hermeneutics is "context is king." I have participated in Christian leadership meetings. One time for a whole week the morning devotion centered upon the parable found later in that same chapter 18 of Matthew. It speaks of forgiveness, and certainly forgiveness is a key element in the gospel. Every day for a week the leader would read portions of this passage and then develop exercises that would help us identify people or situations where we may harbor un-forgiveness. It was interesting, but I could not help but notice they left untouched another deep teaching. Earlier in the chapter the Lord is obviously mentioning heaven and hell. Yet because of fixed concepts and the traditions of men, our group totally dismissed the conclusion of that parable. In addressing the unmerciful servant, "*. . . the master turned him over to the jailers to be tortured, **until** he should pay back all he owed.*" Jesus went on to say, "*This is how my heavenly Father will treat each of you unless you forgive your brother from your heart.*" It was almost like the group collectively agreed, "Yeh right—Like that debt could ever be paid off; Skip that part."

All through scripture we see God is a God of justice and determined punishment for certain offenses. The law regarding "eye for an eye and tooth for a tooth" is based on justice and mercy. I have no right to go beyond the infraction and kill a person to repay him for the loss of my eye. The Mosaic Law speaks of "*purpose driven justice.*" Even the Apostle Paul was shown some level of mercy. Five times he was given the dreaded "forty lashes less one." In their misguided following of the letter of the Law, instead of opening themselves up to the Spirit of the Law, *even* these religious leaders (vipers, hypocrites, whitewashed tombs), show a measure of *purpose driven justice.* Our Constitution and Bill of Rights is based on this Mosaic code of justice and yet traditions of man and a "Hope-less" view of Yahweh, allows us to believe otherwise.

I believe with all my heart that the canon of scripture we call the Holy Bible is divinely inspired.

> *"All Scripture is God-breathed and is useful for teaching, rebuking, correcting, and training in righteousness, so that the man of God may be thoroughly equipped for every good work."*
>
> —2 Tim. 3:16-17

I hope you will agree with me on that point. Would you also say it is likely that in a study group of twenty people, there may be several different translation of the bible? What if words such as *forever, everlasting, eternal,* or *Gehenna* were mistranslated from their original meaning?

Aion

The first of these words is the Greek word, *aion.* It is mostly translated "eternal," "everlasting," and "forever" in the King James Version. However, some translations read "age-abiding," "age-during," or "eon." In the Septuagint, the Greek word *aion* is used to translate the Hebrew word *olam.* Thus, if we want to get a sense of the N.T., we need to understand the meaning of the word, *olam,* in the O.T. Numerous passages referring to *olam* show clearly it cannot mean "never-ending" in those texts. Here are just a few:

- Jonah was in the fish forever (*olam*). But only *until* he left three days later. (Jon. 1:17, 2:6)

- A Moabite is forbidden to enter the Lord's congregation forever (*olam*). But only *until* the 10th generation. (Deut. 23:3)

- A slave serves his master forever (*olam*). But only *until* death ends his servitude. (Ex.21:6)

- The Aronic priesthood is everlasting (*olam*). But only *until* the likeness of Melchizedek arises. (Ex. 40:15; Num. 25:13; Heb. 7:14-22)

Consider these scriptures found in the New Testament using the use of *aion*. Does "eternity" make any sense in the following passages? Here we have translated the Greek word **aion** with the English word "eternity."

- What will be the sign . . . of the end of the **eternity**? (Mt. 24:3)

- Conformed to this **eternity**. (Rom. 12:2)

- Mystery kept secret since the **eternity** began but now made manifest. . . . (Rom. 16:25-26)

- Wisdom of this **eternity**, nor the rulers of this **eternity** . . . ordained before the **eternities** . . . which none of the rulers of this **eternity**. . . . (1 Cor. 2:6-8)

- Deliver us from this present evil **eternity**. (Gal. 1:4)

Scores of passages demonstrated that *aion* is of limited duration. In his book *God's Methods with Man*, the reputable scholar G. Campbell Morgan said:

> Let me say to Bible students that we must be very careful how we use the word "eternity." We have fallen into great error in our constant use of that word. There is no word in the whole Book of God corresponding with our "eternal" which, as commonly used among us, means absolutely without end. The strongest Scripture word used with reference to the existence of God is—"unto the ages of the ages," which does not literally mean eternally.[14]

Gehenna

Another word used in support of the doctrine of everlasting punishment is *Gehenna*. It is one of three words translated *"hell"* in the New Testament. *Gehenna* is not mentioned in the Old Testament or by John, Paul, Peter, Jude, or James in all their writings (except once indirectly regarding the tongue—James 3:6). Nor is it mentioned in the book of Acts or Hebrews. Jesus uses the term on what seems like only four occasions. (A few times He seems to refer to this judgment but without using the term. Mt. 3:10-12; 7:19; 134:40-50; 25:41.) If *Gehenna* were truly eternal and purposeless agony as claimed, how can such a horrible fate—to which most people are destined—not be warned against everywhere? How can you explain this?

Fatherhood of God

If we accept this harsh and endlessly punitive picture of God as being the creator of mankind, we "throw him under the bus."

Not only do we make God in our own image, but where in the world are we to get an example of fatherhood done right? "*Adam, the son of God*" (Luke 3:38). The genealogy of Yeshua recorded in Luke goes back to Adam, the son of God. Some people may get so mad at me for "poking the bear" regarding their view of hell and yet call me superstitious if I suggest to them that the bible is factual, that there was actually a real Adam and a real Eve! When has God ever disowned Adam, Israel, or the nations? When has He ever ceased to be the Father of all creation?

If God is truly a "Father" as we understand fatherhood, then it further confirms He would only discipline His children for their good, as every loving earthly parent does. How could he even give us guidelines for who should be a worthy candidate for ministry? 1 Timothy 3:4 says, "*He must manage his own family well and see that his children obey him with proper respect.*" Wow God—Only a small handful of your creation—your family—are there with you for all eternity in heaven. Kind of stinks to be you—right?

Ephesians 3:14-15 declares, "*For this reason I kneel before the Father, from whom his whole family in heaven and on the earth derives its name.*" Wow God—how does that feel to have the world think you're a pretty lousy father? You either sent all these billions of souls to hell or they ran away from home to get away from you. Kind of stinks to be you—right?

You may be wondering, if these things are true, then where did we get such deep-seated notions and traditions? I explained in earlier chapters that we can thank Emperor Constantine in large part for making sweeping changes to the **faith of our fathers.** Of course there are always a remnant of voices that try to resist apostasy and compromise. In like manner, we can thank St. Augustine, considered by many to be a pillar and true church father, for setting a match to bad doctrine and personal agenda.

The theologian most responsible for establishing this teaching was Augustine in the 5th century. He was not a native Greek speaker. He said, "I have learned very little of Greek language." Is it surprising that a "non-Greek" speaker would misunderstand the Greek words of Scripture? I hope I have made a good case that we as Christians have missed so much truth by our rejection or disregard for our Jewish roots.

Regarding Augustine (354–430 A.D.), Charles Pridgeon wrote, "His influence, probably more than that of any other of the Church Fathers brought forward and emphasized the doctrine of never-ending punishment." Pridgeon quotes Augustine:

> And now I see I must have a gentle disputation with certain tender hearts of our own religion, who are unwilling to believe that everlasting punishment will be inflicted, either on all those whom the just Judge shall condemn to the pains of hell, or even on some of them, but who think that after certain periods of time, longer or shorter according to the proportion of their crimes, they shall be delivered out of that state.
>
> —Augustine[15]

And in *Encheririd, ad Laurent*, Pridgeon again quotes Augustine: "There are very many in our day, who though not denying the Holy Scriptures, do not believe in endless torments."

This may seem just a bit of dusty history to you, but people do funny things when they believe funny things. We can actually become a bit like our interpretation of the gods we serve. Is it any stretch to believe some of the brutalities of the historical Inquisition were done with some sense of religious satisfaction?

Torture and punishment during the Spanish Inquisition

Torture was used only to get a confession and wasn't meant to actually punish the accused heretic for his crimes. Some inquisitors used starvation, forced the accused to consume and hold vast quantities of water or other fluids, or heaped burning coals on parts of their body. But these methods didn't always work fast enough for their liking.

The **rack** was a well-known torture method associated with inquisition. The subject had his hands and feet tied or chained to rollers at one or both ends of a wooden or metal frame. The torturer turned the rollers with a handle, which pulled the chains or ropes in increments and stretched the subject's joints, often until they dislocated. If the torturer continued turning the rollers, the infidel's arms and legs could be torn off. Often, simply seeing someone else being tortured on the rack was enough to make another person confess.

While the accused heretics were on the rack, inquisitors often applied other torture devices to their bodies. These included heated metal pincers, thumbscrews, boots, or other devices designed to burn, pinch or otherwise mutilate their hands, feet or bodily orifices. Although mutilation was technically forbidden, in 1256 Pope Alexander IV decreed that inquisitors could clear each other from any wrongdoing that they might have done during torture sessions.

Inquisitors needed to extract a confession because they believed it was their duty to bring the accused back to the faith. A true confession resulted in the accused being forgiven, but he was usually still forced to absolve himself by performing **penances**, such as pilgrimages or wearing multiple heavy crosses.[16]

Our precious Savior never ordered anyone to be slaughtered for any reason, especially for hardness of heart against His message, nor for disagreeing with Him on spiritual matters. But—and this is a very big 'but'—pagans regularly move to slaughter their opponents, usually with great relish and hardness of heart. In such slaughters, murder is not enough; rather, before the victim dies, pagans absolutely relish inflicting maximum pain upon their victims. White and Black Magic practitioners believe that the pain inflicted before death transfers great occult power to them; so they try to draw out a person's death as long as possible, inflicting the greatest amount of pain possible before death comes. Skilled Inquisition executioners would bring a victim to the point of death many times, only to stop the torture so the victim could revive so they could be tortured again.

Since so few people today have been taught even the rudiments of history, most do not know what the Inquisition was TRULY like. Most people today have no idea of the rampant barbarism and torture wreaked upon the unfortunate inhabitants of Europe for almost 700 years! Most people have no idea how the entire population was consumed by fear, for a knock on one's door in the middle of the night meant immediate beginning of a torturous death at the hands of the Inquisitors. Try to imagine several **centuries** of such dread! We are distressed if even a decade of our life is rough or does not go as we had envisioned it was supposed to.

Even through this though, there have been voices of dissent and reformation. Martin Luther declared:

> I frankly confess that, for myself, even if it could be, I should not want free-will to be given to me . . . But now that God has taken my salvation out of the control of my own will, and put it under control of His, and promised to save me, not according to my working or running, but according to His own grace and mercy, I have the comfortable certainty that He is faithful

and will not lie to me, and that He is also great and powerful, so that no devils or opposition can break Him or pluck me from Him.[17]

This is neither the time nor the place to go into the relationship between Augustine teaching and Islam. Some people have a false notion that Islam is one of the world's oldest religions. That is just not true. Its roots start around 622 A.D. I have already declared my opinion regarding Islam to being a Judeo-Christian counterfeit. Muhammad was greatly influenced by Jewish merchants, Messianic believers, and Catholic/Augustinian thought in his region at that time. As to our discussion about hell and the afterlife, one may say that Muslims are keeping to the fundamental teaching of the Koran and Muhammad when they carry out Jihad. They believe that immediately upon the righteous death of a faithful follower, that person is assured heaven and paradise. They also believe Allah is Most Merciful. While the world may react to a beheading as barbaric, it was commanded by—and modeled by—their prophet. Beheading is actually more merciful than the tortures described earlier.

Yeshua ha Messiach . . . Jesus the Messiah

Scripture refers to Christ as the Savior of the World. In fact, Yeshua (Jesus) means savior (Matthew 1:21). The Father sent Him as such (1 John 4:14). Though we all give lip service to this title, we actually deny it. We attest instead that Christ is merely the Savior of "some" out of the world. Or again, He is the "wish-to-be" Savior of the world. But if the mass of humanity is lost forever, we can call Him what we will; He is not the Savior of the world. It seems as if each denomination, person, or people group has their own criterion for assurance of salvation. It is very subjective really, and has far more to do with personal experience or comfort than it does with the Word of God.

What is God like? Is He kind? Is He cruel? Is He loving? Is He evil? Is He fair? These are questions that matter, the questions all people want answered. This is no peripheral issue, for it affects our very concept of God. And that affects everything—absolutely everything!

> *"To Him who is able to do exceedingly abundantly above all that we can ask or think."*
> —Eph. 3:20. Wow !!!

Our life experiences shape all of us. As a minister, I have been asked to speak at or conduct a funeral service on several occasions. One time a young woman asked me to conduct a funeral service for her child that was still-born. Can you put yourself in the place of that grieving mother? The child died days before she delivered, but she had to carry it to its term. All the hopes and dreams she had for that child in the months preceding died, along with that life within her. It was not hard to assure her of the heaven awaiting that soul who never saw the light of day.

On another occasion I was asked to perform a service for the family of a man who dropped dead in his kitchen. Forty-six years old and gone. They were not a "church" family. He rarely, if ever, darkened the doors of any assembly. I did not know him from Adam himself. It was not easy to find reasons to comfort the family that immediately he was in a better place and home with Jesus. They could not mention one thing he had done to "earn" a place in heaven; and of course it is not my place to ask them for proofs. But stories of things like how "Joe" loved to play golf and cheer for his team are not mentioned in the "faith Hall of Fame" in the book of Hebrews.

My duties (and privilege) as chaplain of an assisted-living home are also unique. It is different than being the nurse on the maternity ward who is at that stage in life where usually there is great joy and excitement. It is a little different ministering to so many who have gotten rid of most everything that defined their very existence. Home, career, memorabilia, and even independence have had to be let go of with the reality they face. It seems that almost every month somebody I have grown close to, or have learned their life story—takes a turn for the worse and leaves this reality.

Do any of you know someone who has lost a dear one to suicide, overdose or tragedy? Do you know someone who is either dealing with death or about to deal with it? Is there someone you know who is open to the fact that our life is about more than sports, cookbooks, or romance novels? I encourage you who are reading, if my book has touched you, to get several copies and hand them out to those who struggle. Find a way as I have to make others aware of "things that matter" and this Blessed Hope.

> *"He will swallow up death forever and will wipe away tears from all faces."*
>
> —Isaiah 25:8

How will he wipe away all tears in heaven? Will He do it by a magic lobotomy to erase the memory of our lost loved ones in hell, or by His great power and wisdom, in winning the hearts of the rebellious? Between the conflicting theologies of the fifth-century theologian (Augustine) and the Early Church, is it not clear which is most worthy of our glorious God?

I have told you two things in this particular chapter that I purpose to remain true to. Momma told me not to talk (any more) about religion and politics. The second one is that I regret not quite magnifying the power and the will of Jehovah enough in my first book.

The Power of Jah Will

There is really NOTHING like it in this life or the life to come. I wish to close the remainder of this chapter with scripture. My arguments may or may not have convinced you. A certain scripture that explodes on my brain now may not move you. Only the Holy Spirit can draw us or convince us of this Blessed Hope.

Please do not skip through this and then have the nerve to declare I did not back up my position with Scripture. God's word tells us in Phillipians 4:8, "*Finally, brothers and sisters, whatever is true, whatever is noble, whatever is right, whatever is pure, whatever is lovely, whatever is admirable—if anything is excellent or praiseworthy—think about such things.*"

Please do not rush through this section with a yawn like some daily devotional. I encourage you to grab a cup of coffee and let it percolate.

Proclamations of Hope:

Genesis
* 1:31 God (Who declares the end from the beginning —Is. 46:10) saw <u>everything</u> He had made as <u>indeed very good!</u>

- 12:3 "All the families of the earth shall be blessed." (18:18; 22:18; 26:4; 28:14)

- 18:25 "Shall not the Judge of all the earth do right?"

- 26:3-4 He makes an oath to bless all nations.

1 Samuel
- 2:6 "The Lord kills and makes alive; He brings down to the grave (Sheol, rendered "hell" 31 times in the KJV) and brings up."

2 Samuel
- 14:14 "God does not take away life; instead, He devises ways so that a banished person may not remain estranged from Him."

1 Chronicles
- 16:34 "He is good! For His mercy endures forever."

- 16:41 "His mercy endures forever."

Job
- 5:17-18 "Do not despise the chastening of the Almighty. For He bruises, but He binds up; He wounds, but His hands make whole."

- 23:13 "Whatever His soul desires that he does."

- 41:2 "You can do all things; no plan of yours can be thwarted."

Psalms
- 2:8 He receives the nations for an inheritance.

- 13:5 "I trust in your <u>unfailing</u> love."

- 22:27 "<u>All</u> the ends of the world shall . . . turn to the lord. And <u>all the families</u> of the nations shall worship before You."

- 22:29 "<u>All</u> those who go down to the dust shall <u>bow</u> before Him . . . who cannot keep himself alive."

- 30:5 "His anger is but for a <u>moment</u>, His favor is for life; weeping may endure for <u>a night</u>, but joy comes in the morning."

- 33:5 "He loves righteousness and justice ("judgment"—KJV); <u>the earth is full of the goodness of the Lord</u>."

- 49:15 "God will redeem my soul from the power of the grave (Sheol) for He shall receive me." Sheol is rendered "hell" 31 times in the KJV.

- 62:12 "To You, O Lord, belongs mercy; for You render each one <u>according</u> to his work."

- 65:2-3 "To You <u>all flesh will come</u> . . . You will provide <u>atonement</u>."

- 66:3-4 "Through the <u>greatness of Your power Your enemies</u> <u>shall</u> submit <u>themselves</u> to You. All the earth shall worship You and sing praises to you."

- 66:11-12 "You laid affliction on our backs . . . We went through <u>fire</u> . . . but You brought us out to <u>rich fulfillment</u>."

- 67:1-4 "God . . . cause His face to shine upon us, so that Your way may be known on earth, Your salvation among <u>all</u> nations . . . let all the peoples praise You. Oh, let the nations be <u>glad</u> and <u>sing for joy</u>! For You shall <u>judge the people righteously</u>."

- 72:11 "<u>All kings</u> shall fall down before Him; <u>all nations</u> shall serve Him."

- 72:17 "<u>All nations</u> shall call Him blessed."

- 82:8 "O God, judge the earth; for You shall inherit <u>all</u> nations."

- 86:9 "<u>All</u> nations shall come, worship, and glorify Him."

- 86:10 "You are great and do <u>wondrous</u> things."

- 86:13 "Great is Your <u>mercy</u> . . . You have delivered my soul from the depths of <u>Sheol</u>." Sheol is rendered "hell" 31 times in the KJV.

- 89:30-34 God will visit His son's transgression with the rod and stripes. "Nevertheless, My loving-kindness I will not utterly take from him, nor allow My faithfulness to fail, My covenant I will not break, nor alter the word that has gone out of my lips."

- 90:3 "You turn man to destruction, and say, "return . . . .""

- 98:6-9 "Shout <u>joyfully</u> . . . for He is coming to <u>judge</u> the earth. With righteousness He shall judge the world . . . the peoples with equity."

- 102:19-20 "The Lord looked down . . . he viewed the earth, to hear the groans of the prisoners and <u>release</u> those condemned to death."

- 103:8-9 He is merciful and gracious, slow to anger, <u>abounding in mercy.</u> He will not always strive with us, nor keep his anger forever.

- 107:1 "He is good! His mercy endures forever."

- 135:6 "Whatever the Lord pleases <u>He does</u>, in heaven and in earth."

- 136:1-26 "His mercy endures forever." Repeated in each verse!

- 138:4 "<u>All</u> kings of the earth shall praise You, O Lord, when they hear the words of Your mouth."

- 145:7-10 "They shall utter the memory of Your great goodness, and shall sing of Your righteousness. The Lord is <u>gracious and full of compassion</u>, slow to anger and great in mercy. The Lord is <u>good to all</u>, and <u>His tender mercies are over all His</u> works. <u>All</u> your works shall praise You, O Lord."

- 145:14-16 "The Lord upholds <u>all</u> who fall and raises up <u>all</u> who are bowed down. The eyes of all look expectantly to You . . . You open Your hand and satisfy the desire of <u>every living thing.</u>"

Proverbs
- 16:9 "A man's heart plans his way, but the Lord directs his steps."

- 19:11 "There are many plans in a man's heart, nevertheless the Lord's counsel (purpose—RSV) that will stand."

- 20:24 "A man's steps are ordained by the lord, how then can man understand his way?" NAS

Isaiah

- 2:2 In the last days His house shall be established and <u>all</u> nations shall flow into it.

- 14:24 "The lord . . . has <u>sworn</u>, saying, 'Surely, as I have thought, so it shall come to pass, and as I have purposed, so it shall stand.'"

- 14:27 "The Lord of hosts has purposed, and who will annul it? His hand is stretched out, and who will turn it back?"

- 25:6-8 "He will make a feast for <u>all</u> people and destroy the covering cast over <u>all</u> people, and the veil that is spread over <u>all</u> nations. He will swallow up death ("in victory"—KJV) forever, and will wipe away tears from <u>all</u> faces."

- 26:9 "When Your judgments are in the earth, the inhabitants of the world will <u>learn</u> righteousness."

- 40:5 "His glory shall be revealed and all flesh shall see it."

- 45:21-25 "There is no other God besides Me, a just God and a Savior . . . Look to Me, and be <u>saved, all you ends of the earth</u>! . . . I have sworn by Myself; the word has gone out of My mouth in righteousness, and shall not return, that to Me <u>every</u> knee shall bow, <u>every</u> tongue shall take an oath. Surely in the Lord I have righteousness and strength. To Him man shall come, and <u>all</u> shall be ashamed who are incensed against him. In the Lord <u>all</u> the descendants of Israel shall be justified, and shall glory."

- 46:10-11 "Declaring the end from the beginning, and from ancient times things that are not yet done, saying, 'My counsel shall stand, and I will do <u>all</u> my pleasure' . . . Indeed I have spoken it; **I will** also bring it to pass. I have purposed it; **I will** also do it."

- 48:10 "Behold, I have <u>refined</u> you . . . tested you in the <u>furnace</u> of affliction."

- 49:6 "I will also give You as a light to the Gentiles, that You should be my salvation to the ends of the earth."

- 50:2 "Is My hand shortened at all that it cannot redeem? Or have I no power to deliver?"

- 50:2 "All the ends of the earth shall see the salvation of our God."

- 53:10-11 "The pleasure of the Lord shall prosper in is hand, he shall see of the labor (travail—KJV) of His soul, and be <u>satisfied</u>."

- 54:8 "With a little wrath I hid My face from you for a <u>moment</u>; but with everlasting kindness I will have mercy on you, says the Lord, your Redeemer."

- 55:8 "He will <u>abundantly pardon</u>. For His thoughts are not our thoughts, nor are His ways our ways."

- 55:11 "So shall My word be that goes forth from My mouth; it shall not return to Me void, but it <u>shall accomplish</u> what I please, and it shall prosper in the thing for which I sent it."

- 57:16 "I will not contend forever, nor will I always be angry; for the spirit would fail before Me, and the souls which I have made."

Jeremiah

- 3:17 "<u>At that</u> time Jerusalem shall be called The Throne of the Lord, and all the nations shall be gathered to it . . . No more shall they follow the dictates of their evil hearts."

- 10:23 "I know the way of man is not in himself; it is not in man who walks to direct his own steps."

- 23:20 "The anger of the Lord will not turn back <u>until</u> he fully accomplishes the purposes of his heart. In days to come you will understand it clearly."

- 31:33-34 "I <u>will</u> put my law in their minds, and write it on their hearts . . . They all shall know Me . . . For I will forgive their iniquity, and their sin I will remember no more."

- 32:17 "There is <u>nothing</u> too hard for You."

- 32:40 "I <u>will put</u> My fear in their hearts so that they <u>will not depart</u> from Me."

Lamentations

- 3:31-33 "The Lord will not cast off forever. Though He causes grief, yet He will show compassion according to the multitude of <u>His mercies</u>. For He does not afflict willingly, nor grieve . . . men."

Ezekiel

- 16:55 "When your sisters, Sodom and her daughters, return to their former state, and Samaria and her daughters return to their former state, then you and your daughters will return to their former state."

- 18:4 "**All souls are mine**." "Thus will not God provide for all His creation? See 1 Tim. 5:8. Absolutely!

- 36:23 "The nations shall know that I am the Lord . . . when I am hallowed in you before their eyes."

- 36:26 "I will give you a new heart and put a new spirit within you; I will take the heart of stone . . . and give you a heart of flesh."

- 36:27 "I will put My Spirit within you and cause you to walk in My statutes, and you will keep My judgments and do them."

- 36:36 "Then the nations which are left all around you shall know that I . . . will do it."

Daniel
- 4:35 "He does according to His will . . . No one can restrain His hand."

- 7:14 "To Him was given dominion . . . that all peoples, nations, and languages should serve him."

- 9:24 "Seventy weeks are determined . . . to make an end of sins, to make reconciliation for iniquity, to bring in everlasting righteousness." All in due time!

Hosea
- 13:14 "I will ransom them from the power of the grave. (Sheol) . . . O death, I will be your plagues! O grave (Sheol), I will be your destruction."

Joel

- 2:28 "I will pour out My Spirit on <u>all flesh</u>."

Jonah

- 4:2 "You are a gracious and merciful God, slow to anger and abundant in loving-kindness, One who relents from doing harm."

Micah

- 7:18-19 "He does not retain His anger forever, because He delights in mercy . . . and will subdue your iniquities."

Habakkuk

- 1:12 "You have appointed them for <u>judgment</u> . . . marked them for <u>correction</u>."

- 2:14 "The earth will be <u>filled</u> with the knowledge of the glory of the Lord., as the waters cover the sea."

Malachi

- 2:10 "Have we not <u>all</u> one Father? Has not one God created us?"

- 3:6 "I am the Lord, <u>I do not change</u>; therefore you are not consumed, O sons of Jacob."

Matthew

- 5:26 "<u>Assuredly</u> . . . you will by no means get out of thee (Gehenna prison) <u>till</u> you have paid the last penny." Mat. 18:34-35, Luke 12:59.

- 5:44 "Love your enemies . . . that you may be sons of your Father." Will God do less?

- 7:2 "With what judgment you judge, you will be judged; and with the measure you use, it will be <u>measured back to you</u>."

- 9:36-38 "When He saw the multitudes, He was <u>moved with compassion</u> for them, because they were weary and scattered like sheep having no shepherd. Then he said . . . 'the harvest truly is plentiful, but the laborers are few. Therefore pray the Lord . . . to send out laborers into His harvest.'" Note: His concern for them was not their impending doom in hell.

- 12:20-21 "Till He send forth judgment unto victory. And in His name shall the Gentiles trust."

- 18:11 "The Son of Man has come to save <u>that</u> which was lost." How many of the lost are included in the word "that"?

- 18:14 "It is <u>not the will</u> of your Father . . . that one of these little ones should perish."

- 23:1,9 "Jesus spoke to the multitudes and to His disciples . . . One is your Father."

Mark
- 9:49 "<u>Everyone</u> will be <u>purified with fire</u>." (GNT). Everyone!

- 10:26-27 "Who then can be saved? With men it is impossible, but not with God; for with God <u>all</u> things are possible."

Luke
- 2:10 "I bring you good tidings of great joy which will be to <u>all</u> people."

- 3:6 "All flesh shall see the salvation of God."

- 3:38 "Adam, the son of God." This makes God the Father of all humanity.

- 4:18 "He has anointed Me to preach the gospel to the poor . . . sent Me to heal the brokenhearted, to proclaim liberty to the captives and recovery of sight to the blind, to give them beauty for ashes . . . oil of joy for mourning, the garment of praise for the spirit of heaviness." See Is. 61:2-3.

- 9:56 "The Son of Man did not come to destroy men's lives but to save them."

- 15:4 "What man of you, having a hundred sheep, if he loses one of them, does not leave the ninety-nine . . . and go after the one which is lost until he finds it?" Would the Good Shepherd do differently?

John

- 1:7-9 "This man came . . . to bear witness of the Light, that all through him might believe . . . the true Light which gives light to every man coming into the world."

- 1:13 "Born, not . . . of the will of man, but of God." Jah—God's will rules.

- 1:29 "Behold! The Lamb . . . who takes away the sin of the world."

- 3:17 "God did not send His Son into the world to condemn the world, but that the world through Him might be saved." Not "might" but WILL be saved.

- 4:42 "We know that this is indeed the . . . <u>Savior of the world</u>."

- 6:33 "He . . . comes down from heaven and gives <u>life</u> to the world."

- 6:51 "I shall give My flesh . . . for the <u>life of the world</u>."

- 8:12 "I am the light of the <u>world</u>."

- 12:32 "I . . . <u>will</u> draw (drag) all peoples to Myself." What He says HE WILL DO!

- 12:47 "I did not come to judge the world but to save the world."

- 17:4 "I have brought You glory on earth by **<u>completing</u>** the work you gave me to do."

Acts
- 3:21 "Heaven must receive (Jesus) <u>until the times</u> of restoration of all things, which God has spoken by the mouths of all His holy prophets since the world began."

- 3:25-26 "In your seed <u>all</u> the families of the earth shall be blessed. To you first, God . . . sent Him to bless you. In turning away <u>every one</u> of you from your iniquities."

- 10:34 "God shows no partiality."

- 17:28-29 "As some of your own poets have said, 'For we also are His children.' Being then the children of God . . . .'" He was speaking to unbelievers.

Romans

- 2:4 "Do you despise the riches of His goodness, forbearance, and longsuffering, not knowing that the goodness of God leads you to repentance?" (Not terror.)

- 3:3-4 "Will their unbelief make the faithfulness of God without effect? Certainly not!"

- 4:21 "What He had promised He was also able to perform."

- 5:8 "While we were still sinners, Christ died for us."

- 5:17 "For if by the one man's offense death reigned through the one, much more those who receive abundance of grace and of the gift of righteousness will rein in life through the One, Jesus Christ."

- 5:18 "Therefore, as through one man's offense judgment came to all men, resulting in condemnation, even so though one Man's righteous act the free gift came to all men, resulting in justification of life."

- 5:20 "Where sin abounded, grace abounded much more."

- 8:21 "The creation (includes all people) itself also will be delivered from the bondage of corruption into the glorious liberty of the children of God."

- 11:15-16 "If their (Israel) being cast away is the reconciling of the world, what will their acceptance be but life from the dead? For if the first-fruit is holy, the lump (of humanity), is also holy."

- 11:26 "All Israel will be saved . . . He will turn away ungodliness from Jacob." Do you think that it only really means all will be saved if they turn right now??

- 11:29 "The gifts and the calling of God are irrevocable."

- 11:32 "God has committed them all to disobedience, that He might have mercy on **all**."

- 11:33 "Oh, the depth of riches both of the wisdom and knowledge of God! How unsearchable are His judgments and His ways past finding out!"

- 11:36 "Of Him and through Him and to Him are all things."

- 12:21 "Overcome evil with good." God is our model.

- 14:11 "Every knee shall bow to Me, and every tongue shall confess to God."

1 Corinthians

- 3:15 "If anyone's work is burned, he will suffer loss; but he himself will be saved, yet so as through fire."

- 13:8 "Love never fails (ends RSV). God is love." See 1 John 4:8,16.

- 15:22 "For as in Adam all die, even so in Christ **all** shall be made alive."

- 15:23 "But each one (Christ, elect, all men) in his own order." In God's appointed time.

- 15:26 "The last enemy that will be destroyed is death (second death)."

- 15:28 "When all "things" are made subject to Him, then . . . that God may be all in all." In God's due time.

- 15:54 "Death is swallowed up in victory."

2 Corinthians

- 5:14 "If One died for all, then all died." All die to sin in Christ.

- 5:19 "God was in Christ reconciling the world to Himself."

Galatians
- 3:8 "The Scripture, foreseeing that God would justify the Gentiles by faith, preached the gospel to Abraham beforehand, saying, 'In you all the nations shall be blessed.'"

Ephesians
- 1:9-11 "Having made known to us the mystery of **His will**, according to His good pleasure which he purposed in Himself, that in the dispensation of the fullness of the times He might gather together in one all things in Christ, both which are in heaven and which are on the earth—in Him—who works all things according to the counsel of **His will**."

- 2:7 "In the ages to come He might show the exceeding riches of His grace in His kindness toward us in Christ Jesus." Note: Ages to come.

- 3:6 The Gentiles are fellow heirs with Israel. What a glorious truth knowing all Israel will be saved!

- 4:8-10 "When He ascended on high, He led captivity captive, and gave gifts to men, Now this, 'He ascended'—what does it mean but that he also first descended into the lower parts of the earth? He who descended is also the One who ascended far above all the heavens, that he might fill all things."

Philippians
- 2:10-11 "At the name of Jesus <u>every knee will bow</u>, of those who are in heaven, and on earth and under the earth, and that <u>every tongue will confess</u> that Jesus Christ is Lord, to the glory of God the Father." NAS

- 3:21 "He is able even to subdue <u>all</u> 'things' to Himself."

Colossians
- 1:19-20 "It <u>pleased</u> the Father . . . by Him to reconcile all 'things' to himself, by Him, whether things on earth or things in heaven, having made peace through the **blood** of His cross."

1 Timothy
- 1:19-20 "Concerning the faith have suffered shipwreck, of whom are Hymenaeus and Alexander, whom I <u>delivered to Satan</u> that they may <u>learn</u> not to blaspheme."

- 2:3-4,6 "This is good and acceptable in the sight of God our Savior; **Who will have all men to be saved**, and to come unto the knowledge of the truth . . . Who gave Himself a ransom for <u>all</u>, to be testified in due time."

- 4:9-11 "This is a faithful saying and worthy of all acceptance. For to this end we both labor and suffer reproach, because we trust in the living God, who is the Savior of all men, especially (not exclusively) of those who believe. These things command and teach."

- 5:8 "If anyone (God included?) does not provide for his own (all souls are His—Eze. 18:4), and especially for those of his household, he has denied the faith and is worse than an unbeliever." Does God abandon His own forever in torment?

2 Timothy
- 1:9 "God . . . saved us and called us . . . not according to our works, but according to his own purpose and grace which was given to us in Christ Jesus before time began."

- 1:10 "Our Savior Jesus Christ . . . has abolished death and brought life and immortality to light through the gospel."

Titus
- 2:11 "The grace of God has appeared, bringing salvation to all men." NAS

Hebrews
- 2:2 "Every transgression and disobedience received a just reward."

- 2:9 "Jesus . . . tasting death for . . . everyone." CLT

- 2:14-15 "Through death he might destroy him who had the power of death, that is, the devil, and release those (all people) who through fear of death were all their lifetime subject to bondage."

- 7:25 "He is . . . able to save to the uttermost."

- 8:10-11 "**I will** put My laws in their minds and write them on their hearts . . . and they shall be My people . . . for all shall know Me, from the least of them to the greatest."

- 13:8 "Jesus Christ is the same yesterday, today, and forever." Always a Savior!

James

- 1:18 "Of **His own will** He brought us forth . . . that we might be a kind of first-fruits of His creatures."

- 2:13 "Mercy triumphs over judgment." Does this apply to God?

- 5:11 "You have heard of the perseverance of Job and seen the end intended by the lord—that the Lord is very compassionate and merciful." When is God not in control?

1 Peter

- 1:8 "You greatly rejoice with the joy inexpressible and full of glory." NAS

- 2:12 The Gentiles will glorify God in the day of visitation because they observed our good works.

- 3:19-20, 4:6 "He . . . went and preached to the spirits in prison, who formerly were disobedient . . . the gospel was preached also to those who are dead, that they might be judged according to men in the flesh, but live according to God in the spirit."

2 Peter

- 3:8 "With the Lord . . . a thousand years (is) as one day."

- 3:9 "The Lord is not slack concerning His promise . . . but <u>longsuffering</u> toward us, <u>not willing</u> that any should perish but that <u>all</u> should come to repentance." What if that really means what it seems to say? He is NOT WILLING and His will—**will be done!**

1 John

- 2:2 "He . . . is the propitiation for our sins. And <u>not for ours only</u> but also for the <u>whole world</u>."

- 3:8 "The Son of God appeared for <u>this purpose</u>, to destroy the works of the devil."

- 4:14 "The Father has sent the Son as Savior of the world."

Revelation

- 1:17-18 "<u>Fear not; I . . . have the keys</u> of hell and of death."

- 5:13 "<u>Every creature</u> which is in heaven and on the earth and under the earth . . . I heard saying: Blessing and honor and glory and power be to Him who sits on the throne."

- 15:4 "<u>Who shall not</u> fear You, O Lord, and glorify Your name? . . . For <u>all</u> nations shall come and <u>worship</u> before You, for Your judgments have been manifested." WOW

- 20:13 "Death and Hades delivered up the dead who were in them. And they were judged, each one according to his works."

- 21:5 "Behold, I will make <u>**all**</u> things new . . . these words are true and faithful."

- 22:3 "There shall be <u>no more curse</u>."[18]

I hope you have read or will at least refer to all these scriptures. I believe Jehovah's word is alive and active. I know that was a lot of verses to wade through. But do not be surprised if the Holy Spirit brings these and other scriptures to mind or speaks to you in the days ahead, building precept upon precept. I think this may help you view so many things differently: other religions, those you love who have passed, those who have hurt you, and the whole counsel of Scripture.

Is this not the Blessed Hope that the world so desperately needs to hear? Is this not the Good News of great joy that we can take to the entire world?

🦢 🦢 🦢

Brain teaser:

The Merciful King

There once was a king who ruled a vast domain. It was his custom, just once a year, to let a condemned prisoner go free. But this was only on one condition; the king loved brain teasers and he prefaced his proclamation accordingly. If the prisoner could answer the question put before him correctly he was free as a bird. Let me take you there and see if you would be so lucky. The criminal is in one large room. There is one door at each end. In front of each door stood a guard. They did not even have weapons! The king gives the man these clues:

a. Behind one of these doors is instant and certain death. Behind the other door is immediate freedom.

b. One of my guards ALWAYS tells the truth. The other guard ALWAYS tell a lie. Furthermore I will not tell you which is which regarding doors or guards!

c. You are allowed to speak only ONE TIME during this test. You are allowed to go up to either guard you choose and ask a question. After you pose your one question you must act or you will remain jailed for life.

If you ask the right question and then, by all means, do accordingly—I—the mighty and merciful king . . . will watch you set yourself free. The riddle is "What question would you ask?"

Answers in the back.

Chapter 7

End of Times?

*M*omma told me not to talk about religion or politics, but she never said anything about Eschatology. Man, I wish I had something, say like a diamond ring, for every time I have heard the Messiah was coming back in my lifetime. I mean seriously, the bling would blind ya. I've been "Born Again" since around the '70s at least. Right there with the Jesus Movement . . . . Larry Norman singing, "I wish we'd all been ready." When the planets were supposed to line up around 1977—I was lookin' up. We heard preachers and saw charts all proclaiming that we were overdue! I mean, Israel became a nation in 1948. Everybody knows that "this generation shall not pass away" until he comes; and they declare a generation is considered 40 years. So like—Duh!—1988 would be the right time. Nothin! If you're having a garage sale let me know. I have *Left Behind* books and VHS tapes in a cabinet somewhere. I was scuba diving in Cozumel in 1997 when the comet Hale Bopp cruised by. While it was beautiful, it showed no sign of zapping us out of here. How about Y-2K? Remember that? It stood for "Y"awn 2000.

And the years keep rolling by . . . Shemitah—Baleetah. I hope you sense I am saying some of these things for comic effect, especially after what we dealt with in the last chapter. I respect the teaching regarding Shemitah, and yet it may not turn out to be as pivotal as some have reported. With all this in mind, I wonder if this is what the Master spoke about when He said, "When I return will I find faith upon the earth?" I mean it is hard to figure out . . . We here in the West cry out, "O Father, we *just* come before you today and we *just* want to ask you to, like *just*, take us out of here before the tribulation" (or before our retirement portfolio tanks). We wander around with this mentality while much of the world is suffering now . . . wars and rumors of war . . . masses fleeing their countries . . . beheadings and brutality.

Since so many others have spoken or published their opinion regarding End Times, I think I'll take a whack at it. I'm not feeling any real dates as to when Jesus is returning though, so please don't hold your breath. I do, however, have some opinions on the times we live in.

I have spoken about religion more than once in our conversation and specifically about Islam a couple times. Some people get in an uproar over what we consider atrocities in the news about the rising tide of "militant Islam." I have personally known young men who have enlisted in the armed forces and now just wish the country would declare some kind of war so they could go give 'em you know what (Sheol or Gehenna). You cannot go a day without seeing all manner of hatred toward them on our "National Homeroom Board"—Facebook!! We are just waiting until some form of Christian Force rises up and puts an end to those "Evildoers." I want to go on record here as saying I think there may be an unexpected outcome to much of this. I agree that the persecution and terrorism that is largely coming from Muslim areas is a plague. I believe that it will be dealt with. Our God is a just God and he hears the cries of his martyrs and the persecuted church. I will not be surprised when there is perhaps a nuclear conflict involving Sunni against Shia sects of Islam. I will also expect that our friends Israel (the size of New Jersey) will rise up in the favor of Jehovah and experience supernatural victories. (You should read some of the miraculous accounts from the Six-Day War.)

But rather than the West (and certainly the Church of the West) going back to her compromising and apathetic ways, I feel there will be a very real outcome. We who are Christian are soon to be an apolitical group. With the outcry and disgust with Muslim fanaticism will come a similar disgust with any true believer. We who are fundamental (fundamentally believe Jesus is Lord) will be looked on as intolerant and dangerous. We will not fit in and the "separation" . . . (holiness) will become more and more apparent. We who are "citizens of another Kingdom" will be excluded from the *party*. I know this flies in the face of those who preach we are about to prosper as never before, or those who lean toward "Kingdom Now—Dominion Theology" and feel we'll just get more and more triumphant until we just kind of turn over the wheel to Jesus and let him "take us on home." A calling to "return to innocence" also carries with it a call to not think ourselves as greater than the Master.

> *"Blessed are they which are **persecuted** for righteousness' sake: for theirs is the kingdom of heaven. Blessed are you, when men shall revile **you**, and **persecute you**, and shall say all manner of evil against you falsely, for **my sake**.*

143

Rejoice, and be exceeding glad, for great is your reward
in the heavens."

(Emphasis mine)   —Matt. 5:11

Remember the scripture that declares evil will be called good
and good evil in Isaiah 5:20?

*"But mark this: There will be terrible times in the last days.
People will be lovers of themselves, lovers of money, boast-
ful, proud, abusive, disobedient to their parents, ungrateful,
unholy, without love, unforgiving, slanderous, without
self-control, brutal, not lovers of the good, treacherous,
rash, conceited, lovers of pleasure rather than lovers of
God—having a form of godliness but denying its power."*
—2 Tim. 3:1-5

Remember back to our lesson on Early Church history. They
turned the *then known* world upside down. But their greatest
growth came during persecution and distress.

🦆 🦆 🦆

I said in the beginning of this book that I believe one thing
(probably one of several things) that Yahweh seems to be trying
to convey to His church is that of returning toward our Jewish
roots. I am convinced there is one more. It goes along with the
title of this chapter and the End of Times. This too has definite
connection with our Hebrew roots:

*"Remember that at that time you were separate from
Christ, excluded from citizenship in Israel and foreigners*

*to the covenants of the promise, without hope and
without God in the world. But now in Christ Jesus you
who once were far away have been brought near by the
blood of Christ.*

*For he himself is our peace, who has made the two groups
<u>one</u> and has destroyed the barrier, the dividing wall of
hostility, by setting aside in his flesh the law with its
commands and regulations. His purpose was to create
in <u>himself</u>, **one new man** . . . ."*

(Emphasis mine)   —Eph. 2:12-15

This formation of the "One New Man" is where I think we
are now in the Body of Christ. This concept of "one new man"
in Hebrew basically translates as *am echad hadash* a "new united
people" or "a single new humanity." I have spent a lot of time in
this book talking about our Jewish roots as well as the Gentile
church and our traditions. In my opinion, both sides need to
kind of "get over themselves." There are many people who want
to take us back to looking and acting like historic Jews (often the
unsaved kind). And there are also too many who think this Gentile
church—this Romanized church—is the one new concept and
God's true model. Remember we spoke about the Hebrew Shema,
Adonai Echad, and the unique "oneness" of the Godhead. I also
said that Moses uses that same word *Echad*, when he is describing
how the man and woman become <u>one</u> flesh. Keep this in mind
when you allow Jehovah to mold you into the Kingdom person he
desires, mystically designed and balanced . . . perfect (complete)
for every good work.

145

Let me explain what this has to do with End Times as well as the End of Times. Have you ever heard the expression, "the fullness of the Gentiles?"

The Times of the Gentiles:

Romans 11:25 I do not want you to be ignorant of this . . .

*"I do not want you to be ignorant of this mystery, brothers, so that you may not be conceited: Israel has experienced a hardening in part until the **full number of the Gentiles** has come in."*

What is that full number of the Gentiles? Is it 144,000? How many millions or billions is it? If Billy Graham's estimation of only a *small percentage of church members are saved*, then how are we ever going to get the quota? Does Jehovah have a certain number in mind?

Matthew 24:14 And this gospel of the kingdom will be . . .

"And this gospel of the kingdom will be preached in the whole world as a testimony to all nations, and then the end will come."

Maybe now with the advent of the internet we will finally be able to reach all people groups with the gospel. Maybe now we can come in with some better stats for the Kingdom.

Luke 21:24 They will fall by the sword and will be taken as . . .

*"They will fall by the sword and will be taken as prisoners to all the nations. Jerusalem will be trampled on by the Gentiles until **the times of the Gentiles are fulfilled**."*

I explained in our last chapter that we have gotten some misunderstanding of God due to poor or inaccurate translations of the original wording. I think this may be another case of that. Having a grasp of the words Paul used helps us to better understand

146

this "Mystery of Israel." Some Bible versions (NIV) translate this phrase *until the full number of the Gentiles has come in*. This is unfortunate, and is more of a paraphrase than a translation.

*** If Paul had meant to say *full number* he could have used a different Greek word: *arithmou*, as in Revelation 7:4, "the" *number of those who were sealed*; or *telestoi*, "full number of days," even as Luke used in Luke 1:43 (NASB).

*** Paul used the word *pleroma*, and it is never translated anywhere else as full number, but only as "fullness" (as 11:12). Paul meant fulfilled as in "complete, the state of being full." In its verb form, *pleroma* means "to be full, or filled up," thus *the fullness of the Gentiles has come in* refers to the yielding of Gentile believers to God's will. The result of this will be the salvation of Israel.

Let me quote another source for this next part:

Is 'The Church' Israel?

So, just what does fullness of the Gentiles mean? There are three prominent views to be considered. First, some say that the 'Church' is Israel; thus the fullness of the Gentiles refers to the glory of the Church. The idea that the Church replaces Israel is sometimes called 'replacement theology.' This view of the glory of the Church is incorrect for several reasons.

First, not only is this view grammatically impossible, it is contextually impossible. All the way through Romans 11, "Israel" is referred to as the Jewish people, and distinct from the Gentile believers (vv. 2,7,25,26). Also, it is redemptively impossible. In 11:25, it says blindness in part has happened to Israel, but of the Church Paul says that the eyes of our understanding have been enlightened as to who Messiah is (Ephesians 1:18). Thus the Church as Israel being blind simply makes no sense. Plus, in Romans 11:26 a 'saved Israel' is equated with a 'delivered Jacob:' . . . The Deliverer will come from Zion, He will remove ungodliness from Jacob. The Church, which is not spoken about in this chapter, is made up of those already redeemed, both Jews and Gentiles. Here blinded Israel is spoken of as one that is not yet redeemed but will be. Finally, the view of the glory of the Church is thematically impossible. The whole theme and purpose of Romans 9-11 is to show God's faithfulness to the Jewish people who are Israel (see Romans 9:3,4); it simply does not speak of Israel being replaced by, or identified as the Church.

It's The Rapture, Right?

The second view sees the fullness of the Gentiles referring to the completion of, or Rapture of, the Church. This view maintains that when God fills His quota of Gentiles, and these multitudes are 'brought in' or saved, this is the fullness of the Gentiles. In other words, when the last Gentile is saved, then the Rapture takes place (see 1 Thessalonians 4:16-5:5), at which point God begins working among the Jews again. One reason this falls short is that it assumes the body of Messiah is made up of Gentiles only. But the Body of Messiah is made up of Jews and Gentiles, co-equals in the Lord. And for all we know, the last person saved before the Rapture might be a Jew!

Fulfilling God's Will

The third view held by a growing number of Messianic and other evangelical believers sees the fullness of the Gentiles as referring to the faithfulness of the Gentile believers. In Romans 11:12 how much more their [Israel's] fullness? The word fullness has to do with the completion of Israel's calling, as opposed to their transgression and failure to do God's will (vv. 12,30). Thus the fullness of the Gentiles means Gentile believers will be faithful to fulfill their calling toward Israel: to make Israel jealous.[19]

I could be wrong in venturing that there is yet one more explanation regarding the "times of the Gentiles." I have tried to take us back to Yahweh's *original intent*. It never was about having a religion; it always has and always will be about his having a people . . . ONE person at a time. So many teachers call this age we are in now to be the "church age." That sounds so self-centered to me. It is as if he never had much of a plan until the time of Acts and his church was born. But was it? I maintain that God has always had a people. It started as a person, Adam. It grew and grew, person by person throughout the Old Testament. I have to cut out too many scriptures in my Old Testament to not believe he has always had a people. He has always had a remnant. There are too many scriptures, in Psalms alone, that cry out, "Do not take your presence from me" . . . and . . . "Take not your spirit from me." There are too many instances where the Patriarchs knew that the Spirit of Jehovah was with them . . . and would never leave them. So I believe God always had a people, an assembly. I rejoice though that now we can be a people with the indwelling Spirit of the Lord to lead us. We carry within us what the prophets only dreamed of and sensed was a coming promise.

In my opinion the term "times" means more than number. *Times* is a God ordained season, if you will, a turn in the drama of His-story. We have two words for "time" in the Greek alone. One is *chronos* . . . and that is from where we get our word chronology.

The time is two o-clock. The other Greek word for time—that special God ordained time—is *kairos*.

> *"But when the **time** had <u>fully</u> come, God sent his Son, born of a woman . . ."*
>
> —Galatians 4:4

This had nothing to do with 9:15 Bethlehem Standard time. This was that *kairos*—God-ordained—time that had been prophesied about for so long. It was the exact time when our Savior was destined to fulfill all that the Father had PURPOSED. **Jah Will!**

> *"And He made known to us the mystery of his will (**JAH will–**) according to his good pleasure, which he purposed (**JAH purposed–**) in Christ, to be put into effect when the **times** (–kairos–) will have reached their fulfillment—to bring all things in heaven and on earth together under **one head**, even Christ."*
>
> (Emphasis mine)   —Ephesians 1:9-10

I spoke to you many words ago asking if the Son of Man had a place to lay his head . . . . His authority. I am speaking to you now that we, as the Bride of Christ, are his body. He is the head . . . . In him we can grow to be that One New Man.

We, the Gentile church, have had our "set time" on the stage of God's plan. We were called to make Israel jealous. I'm afraid we have not done a great job of that. The Jews had their purpose. Part of their purpose was to usher in the Law, which speaks of Yeshua and of heavenly things. But they rejected their Messiah. The Gentiles, and specifically the Gentile Church, have now had our turn. We have known the fullness of the Spirit in ways they could not. But I'm afraid, on the whole, we have rejected our Jewish roots. We broke fellowship with our brothers. We have had wonderful outpourings of his Spirit and certainly his mercy, even with our mixture and compromise.

If the Church of Messiah has to go "underground," and I believe it will, it is more than time for the One New Man to arise. That will be a Kingdom man. Complete and well-grafted. One that will respond to the leading of Ruah ha Kodesh . . . Spirit (Divine Breath) that is Holy. I believe that the times of the Gentiles have been, or are being, fulfilled. The fullness of the Gentiles is complete.

Some teach that today is the day of "new wineskins." There are many wonderful teachings on this subject. I have suggested that I believe that this is the time for the "one new man" to arise. Let me also leave you with an idea of just what that "Kingdom man—or woman" will look like. I have been an admirer of Watchman Nee for several decades. He was a devoted follower of Christ and that devotion cost him his life. He died in a Chinese prison in 1972 after being locked up for 15 years. His writings are not an "easy read," as he writes with both maturity and authority. It was after reading his book *"The Normal Christian Life,"* that I stepped out of a comfortable and secure *career boat* and onto the *waters of faith*, and my life was never the same. I wish to quote him as I paint a picture of our "new man" and Kingdom life:

> *Every true servant of God must know at some time that disabling from which he can never recover; he can never be quite the same again. You will fear to move out on the impulse of your soul, for you know what a bad time you*

will have in your own heart before the Lord if you do. You have known something of the chastening hand of a loving God upon you, a God who deals with you as with sons (Heb. 12,7). The Spirit Himself bears witness in your spirit to that relationship, and to the inheritance and glory that are ours 'if so be that we suffer with him' (Rom. 8:16,17); and your response to the Father of our spirits is, 'Abba, Father.'

When the body becomes our life we live like beasts. When the soul becomes our life we live as rebels and fugitives from God—gifted, cultured, educated no doubt, but alienated from the life of God. But when we come to live our life in the Spirit and by the Spirit, though we still use our soul faculties just as we do our physical faculties, they are now the servants of the Spirit; and when we have reached that point God can really use us.

'Lord, I am willing to let go of all this for You; not just for Your work, not for Your children, not for anything else at all, but altogether and only for Yourself.' . . . Oh, to be so wasted! It is a blessed thing to be wasted for the Lord. So many who have been prominent in the Christian world know nothing of this. Many of us have been used to the full—have been used, I would say, too much—but we do not know what it means to be wasted on God. We like to be always on the go; the Lord would prefer to have us in prison. We think in terms of apostolic journeys; God dares to put His greatest ambassadors in chains.[20]

I did not include the above comments from Watchman Nee to scare you, nor to diminish the joys and the victories that are ours in Messiah. But we are told that, in these last and confusing days, many will come in the name of Christ. We are told in Scripture that many will do great and wonderful miracles; but Messiah will say, "Depart—I never KNEW you." We had better get a clear image of the real so as not to chase in vain after the counterfeit! He is calling to us. Do you sense it?

> *"The Spirit and the bride say, 'Come!' And let him who hears say, 'Come!' Whoever is thirsty; let him take the free gift of the water of life."*
> —Revelation 22:17

It would not be uncommon for an author to now give some sort of invitation. Perhaps someone who is reading this has never made a decision for the Messiah and I should not miss this opportunity. In *The Power of I Will*, I show us the incredible power of our own free will. There is really nothing we can give the Father other than our belief in Him. "*Abraham believed God and it was credited to him as righteousness*" (James 2:23). The truly neat thing about grasping

The Power of Jah Will

is this: If you really get it and start to believe what scripture tells us, you know that He WILL have his way. He does know how to lovingly ordain our steps. He WILL never stop until we all are complete in him. The scripture tells us that only a fool says in his heart that there is no God. We are told that the beginning of wisdom is the fear (healthy awe) of the Lord. No matter who you are, reading this now, we all can draw closer to him. If you really believe the scripture, *"If I be lifted up (and He was on the cross) I will draw all men unto me"* (Emphasis mine)   John 12:32. It's going to happen. We can surrender to him and learn to live Kingdom life here on earth—now—or we can be drawn and learn it in the ages (eternities) to come . . . . the hard way. That is what I am excited about. I know and love the scriptures. I am totally convinced that He is, and He is, the rewarder of those who seek him. But what I need is to learn of His Kingdom and His power—the kind of power the early church moved in. Scripture says that signs and wonders followed them wherever they went. Scripture also clearly tells us that the greatest of all gifts is LOVE. This is the quest that I am on. Let us endeavor to **enjoy** the journey!

~ Come with me . . . Return to innocence ~

I dedicated this book to my wife and to you. Will you let me pray this benediction over you as we part?

> *O Father, You are the Most High. You are deserving of all praise and honor. Blessed be the Elohim and Father of our Master Yeshua the Messiah. Thank you Jah, that you have called us saints. You have declared that we are a holy people and a royal priesthood, and citizens of your Kingdom. We bless you O Father, You who have blessed us with every spiritual blessing in heaven through Messiah, even as You have elected us in Him before the foundation of the world. You have called for us to be holy and without blemish before You in love. You have marked us with Your love to be His from the beginning and adopted us to be sons through Yeshua our Messiah, according to how it pleased Your will. O Abba, give us the spirit of wisdom*

and revelation in the full knowledge of You. Let the eyes of our mind be enlightened, that we would know what is the hope of Your calling, and what are the riches of the glory of Your inheritance in the saints. Let us know and walk in the surpassing greatness of Your power toward us, the ones believing according to the working of Your mighty strength.

For this reason I kneel before the Father, from whom His whole family in heaven and on earth derives its name. I pray that out of Your glorious riches You may strengthen us with power through Your Spirit in our inner being so that Messiah may dwell in our hearts through faith. I pray that we, being rooted and established in love, may have power together with all the saints to grasp how wide and long and high and deep is the love of Yeshua. May we know this love that surpasses knowledge—that we may be filled to the measure of all the fullness of our Elohim. Now to Him who is able to do immeasurably more than all we ask or imagine, according to His great power that is at work within us; to Him be glory in the church and in Yeshua our Messiah throughout all generations for ever and ever! Amen.

—(Paraphrased from 1 Pet. 2:9 . . . 2 Cor. 1:3 . . . Eph. 1:4,18-19; 3:14-20)

Bibliography

[1] Bunting, Joe, http://thewritepractice.com/why-we-write/, 2012

[2] Ibid.

[3] Broughton, Barry A., PhD, Grandmaster/Founder, "AKT Combatives"

[4] Eddy, Dr. Charles, W, *The Power of I Will*, Pilgrim-Way, 2011

[5] Names of Jehovah—Jah or Yah, https://en.wikipedia.org/wiki/Jah

[6] Justler, Dan, (From his message given at Glory of Zion Outreach Center in Denton, Texas, Oct. 8, 2000)

[7] Basilica, https://simple.wikipedia.org/wiki/

[8] Heidler, Dr. Robert D., *Messianic Church Arising*, Glory of Zion Ministries, 2006
Note: I asked and received permission from the author for this section of my book. I highly recommend you get his book. It is the most balanced work on Jewish roots and church history combined that I have ever read.

[9] Howey, Paul, *Traditions of Men,* http://www.truthguard.com/Articles/the-danger-of-the-traditions-of-men-a6.html

[10] "God Hates Religion," http://definingthenarrative.com/god-hates-religion

[11] Dore, Gustave, "Images of Hell," https://www.google.com/search?q=dore+illustrations+of+hell&rlz

[12] Hymers, Dr. R. L. Jr., *A Warning To All Who Think They Are Saved,* http://www.rlhymersjr.com/Online_Sermons/03-24-01_A_Warning_to_Those_Who_Think_They_Are_Saved.htm, 2001

[13] Johnson, William. J, *Abraham Lincoln the Christian,* Milford, MI: Mott Media, 1976

[14] Morgan, G. Campbell, *God's Methods with Man,* New York, Revell, 1898

[15] Pridgeon, Charles H., *Is Hell Eternal—Will God's Plan Fail?,* Third Ed. 1931

[16] *Torture and Punishment,* http://history.howstuffworks.com/historical-figures/spanish-inquisition3.htm

[17] Dillenberger, John Ed., *Martin Luther: Selections from His Writings,* New York, Garden City, 1961

[18] Beauchemin, Gary, *Hope Beyond Hell,* Proclamations of Hope, Olmito Texas, Malista Press, 2007 *Note: I received permission from the author to use his book in any manner that would glorify God. I highly recommend you order his book for yourself and visit his website. His work is the most complete I have ever found on this Blessed Hope! http://www.hopebeyondhell.net/

[19] Nadar, Sam, *Jewish Evangelism and Discipleship, The fullness of the Gentiles—What it really Means*

[20] Watchman, Nee, *The Normal Christian life,* Christian Literature Crusade, 1957

Answers to brain teasers:

Chapter 1

I have two coins in my pocket. They total thirty-five cents . . . .
US currency, by the way. One of the coins is NOT A DIME. What
are the two coins in my pocket?

"So what? The other one is a dime. I have a quarter and a dime.

(Please come back for another)

Chapter 2

I live in a part of the United States near Niagara Falls. It is actually one of the great wonders of the world. Each year countless
people visit from all over the world to take in the sight. What
you may not know is that this area is also the border between the
United States and the nation of Canada. Sometimes people pay
to take a helicopter ride to view the majestic falls and of course
an international border. You may have not heard the tragic news
recently. The pilot lost control and that helicopter went down
RIGHT on the border. My question to you is this: in what country
did they most likely bury the survivors?

"Seriously? What country do you come from? Who buries survivors?"

(Please come back for another dose)

Chapter 3

One thing I really love to do is scuba dive. For that matter, I just love being near the ocean. Oh man, to be out on a boat, riding the waves with the wind and sea splashing over the bow, to feel the sun on my skin—now that's a good day. I noticed another boat in the harbor as we were getting ready to go out to sea. It had a ladder over the side like many boats do. It looked like an aluminum ladder with rungs one foot apart. This boat had what appeared to be a 10-foot ladder and the water came up to the second rung. The tide comes in at the rate of one-half foot per hour in that coastal area. My question is this: how many hours will it take for the water to **touch** the fifth rung?

"One cool thing that makes a boat a boat and not an anchor—it floats!"

(I know you'll like the next one.)

Chapter 4

I have to go to market to sell my products. I live in a rather rural area you see and I am a bit of a gentleman farmer. I have three items that I can manage to carry or herd, but there still remains a problem. I have a fox, a rabbit, and a head of lettuce. The market is just across a lazy but deep river and I must hire a ferry to get myself to market. Here's the rub—The ferry operator is like a mean ogre. He will allow me to only carry one item at a time across the river. Man, he's a greedy jerk! So my problem is this: how do I get my entire product to market—each one in good condition to fetch the best price?

"Let's not have anything gobbled up. Take the rabbit across. Come back and get the lettuce. Take the lettuce over, set it down, and pick up the rabbit and bring it back with you. Put rabbit down and pick up fox and take it across. Come back and pick up der bunny and cross over on your way to market. Good luck."

Chapter 5

You are doing well on your journey so far young Jedi. Please take a moment to practice your skill with an easy riddle. You will need the force to be strong with you for the one at the end of the next chapter.

Can you name three consecutive days without using the words Wednesday, Friday, or Sunday?

"Yesterday, today, and tomorrow."

Chapter 6

The Merciful King

There once was a king who ruled a vast domain. It was his custom, just once a year, to let a condemned prisoner go free. But this was only on one condition; the king loved brain teasers and he prefaced his proclamation accordingly. If the prisoner could answer the question put before him correctly he was free as a bird. Let me take you there and see if you would be so lucky. The criminal is in one large room. There is one door at each end. In front of each door stood a guard. They did not even have weapons! The king gives the man these clues:

    a. Behind one of these doors is instant and certain death. Behind the other door is immediate freedom.

b. One of my guards ALWAYS tells the truth. The other guard ALWAYS tells a lie. Furthermore I will not tell you which is which regarding doors or guards!

c. You are allowed to speak only ONE TIME during this test. You are allowed to go up to either guard you choose and ask a question. After you pose your one question you must act or you will remain jailed for life.

If you ask the right question and then, by all means, do accordingly—I—the mighty and merciful king . . . will watch you set yourself free. The riddle is "What question would you ask?"

"You go up to either guard (it matters not) and ask him this question. 'If I were to ask the other guard which door leads to the road to freedom, which one would he tell me' . . . Then you go to the opposite door and freely leave."

About the Author

One place in the book we mention that everyone has what is called a worldview, "from a grave-digger to a graduate student." The author can say that he has held both of those positions. If we live long enough, and by God's blessing, we can play many roles. I have enjoyed being a son, husband and father. Other stops on the journey have included high school teacher and coach . . . business owner for over two decades . . . building contractor . . . ordained minister . . . faith-based counselor . . . and missionary to several countries.

Please visit our website at *www.journey-man.org*. The author is available for speaking engagements upon request. For more information you can also contact *pilgrimceddy@yahoo.com*. We would love to hear from you. We look forward to hearing how God has led you to awesome new areas of life and His will.

Some proceeds of the sale of this book will go directly to helping the needy souls in India. We are trying to complete our AFM Children's Home as well as Messianic Bible College and would desire your help if so moved.

www.ingramcontent.com/pod-product-compliance
Lightning Source LLC
LaVergne TN
LVHW011231080426
835509LV00005B/434